New York Times Bestselling Author
Diana von Welanetz Wentworth
Co-Authored by
Lady JB Owen

Expect
Magic

Transforming Life's Ordinary
Into the Extraordinary.

Publisher's Note: Ignite Publishing is proud and excited to bring you this book by *New York Times* best-selling author Diana von Welanetz Wentworth, *Expect Magic.*

As the leader in Empowerment publishing, Ignite's mission is to produce inspiring, motivational, and empowering books that will Ignite the reader's life. They are of the highest caliber to offer engaging, profound, and life-changing information that will impact the reader. Our mandate is to build a conscious, positive, and supportive community through our books, speaking events, writing workshops, Ignite experiences, podcasts, TV shows, and marketplace. We welcome new book ideas and new authors onto our platform. Should you desire to be published, please apply at www.igniteyou.life/apply or reach out to us at info@igniteyou.life.

Published and printed by Ignite Publishing™, a division of JBO Global Inc.
5569-47th Street Red Deer, AB
Canada, T4N1S1

Cover design by JB Owen and Brent Casteling
Book design by JB Owen and Kristine Magno
Edited by JB Owen, Mimi Safiyah, and Carissa Simpson
Designed in Canada, Printed in China
ISBN: 979-8-9910888-1-7
First edition:© February, 2025

Ordering Information: Quantity sales. Special discounts are available on quantity purchases by corporations, associations, and others. For details, contact the publisher at the above address. Programs, products, or services provided by the author are found by contacting them directly. Resources named in the book are found in the resources pages at the back of the book.

Author Details:
Diana von Welanetz Wentworth   Lady JB Owen
www.DianaWentworth.com   www.jbowen.website

NUCALM is a trademark of SOLACE LIFESCIENCES, INC.

ZOOM is a trademark of Zoom Video Communications, Inc.

References

Poem "Give It All Away" by Pastor Steve Garnaas-Holmes www.unfoldinglight.net

Thank you to Daniel Ladinski for granting permission to use his beautiful Hafiz translations in my blogs and books.

Other Books By Diana

Send Me Someone: A True Story of Love Here and Hereafter (Renaissance Books, 2001)

Chicken Soup for the Soul Cookbook: Recipes and Stories from the Heart co-authored with Jack Canfield and Mark Victor Hansen (Health Communications, 1995)

The Pleasure of Your Company: Elegant "Come to Dinner" Recipes and Menus for a Couple or a Crowd (Atheneum, 1976) (Cookbook of the Year Award)

Chicken Soup to Inspire the Body and Soul: Motivation for Living and Loving a Healthy Lifestyle co-authored with Jack Canfield, Mark Victor Hansen, and Dan Millman (Health Communications, 2012)

With Love From Your Kitchen: Good Things to Make and Give (J. P Tarcher, 1976)

The Art of Buffet Entertaining (J. P. Tarcher, 1978)

The von Welanetz Guide to Ethnic Ingredients: How to Buy and Prepare More than 1000 Foods from Around the World (J. P. Tarcher, 1983)

L.A. Cuisine: the New Culinary Spirit: Recipes and Menus from the Celebrated Chefs of Los Angeles (J. P. Tarcher, 1985)

Celebrations: A Menu Cookbook for Informal Entertaining (J. P. Tarcher, 1978)

Women Gone Wild: Wealth; The Feminine Guide to Living Fearless with Rhonda Swan (Brown Books Publishing Group, 2023)

Love Your Heart: Follow the Red Thread to a Heart-Centered Life (Enlightenment Lifestyle Press, 2013)

Endorsements

"Expect Magic is a marvelous and beautifully written book for anyone searching for more meaning and personal fulfillment in these challenging times. Diana's compassionate insight and timeless understandings have emerged from her own lifetime of deep spiritual experience and created a loving guide that is both practical and profoundly uplifting. She is a magical human being whose journey will inspire you, strengthen you, and bring more joy to your own path of discovery and transformation."

— Dr. Barbara De Angelis
#1 NY Times Bestselling Author and Transformation Teacher

•————•

"My lifelong friend, Diana, is a master at creating, expressing, and sharing the idea that we can EACH innovate infinitely more now. She makes life endlessly exciting moment-by-magic moment. Read, enjoy, absorb, and share this phenomenal book."

—Mark Victor Hansen
American inspirational and motivational speaker, trainer, and NY Times bestselling author. He is best known as the founder and co-creator of the *Chicken Soup for the Soul*™ book series.

•————•

"Expect Magic is a piece of art weaving Diana's personal wisdom and story together with the best, most workable tips to create a life that breathes magic and synchronicity. Here's a secret: Magic is soon to become the new normal without ever dimming its light and joy. Diana is the perfect messenger for this revelation."

—Penney Peirce
Author of *Transparency, Leap of Perception,* and *Frequency.*

•————•

"Diana Wentworth has been on the inside edge of transformation and personal growth for decades. She knows the terrain in which magic is seeded, cultivated, and achieved. Pay attention, follow her suggestions, and ... poof! ... enjoy what you manifest."

—PHILIP GOLDBERG
Author of *American Veda* and *Spiritual Practice for Crazy Times*

Expect Magic Testimonials

"It warms my heart to know my friend Diana has written a book that so many will benefit from. Her insight into expecting magic is so needed at this time when many feel lost and hopeless. The reader will find magic in unexpected ways that will enrich their lives."

—JOYCE BULIFANT
American actress and author, known for her roles in *The Mary Tyler Moore Show*, *The Happiest Millionaire*, and *Airplane!*

⸺•⸺

"When I first picked up this book, I braced myself, "Oh no, not another pop-psychology book full of empty platitudes and feel-good fluff." I couldn't have been more wrong. Diana doesn't just talk about magic—she reveals it. She distills its essence, showing you that when you expect magic, you invite it into your life. Simple? Yes, and very profound. With depth, clarity, and a touch of wonder, she unveils the elements that make magic real—not just in fleeting moments, but as a guiding force in your life. This book is magic. It will inspire you and it will transform the way you see the world. Diana, you are a different kind of magician. You don't just perform the magic—you show us how it works, how it's always been there, and how we, too, can become magicians in our own lives. By the time I turned the last page, one thought filled my mind, "I need to read this again." How many books have ever made you feel that way?

— MARTIN RUTTE,
Founder: www.ProjectHeavenOnEarth.com

⸺•⸺

"Expect Magic! is a heartfelt masterpiece that captures the extraordinary beauty hidden in life's everyday moments. Diana Wentworth's personal stories and profound insights inspire readers to open their hearts to synchronicity and embrace the limitless possibilities around them. This book feels like a warm conversation with a dear friend, gently reminding us to expect miracles and rediscover the magic within ourselves and the world. It's a treasure for anyone seeking inspiration and transformation."

—RHONDA SWAN
CEO of Unstoppable Branding Agency & Founder of
Women Gone Wild Book Series

⸺•⸺

"With Expect Magic, Diana von Welantz Wentworth has once again shown why she's a brilliant New York Times best-selling author of ten books. In this latest work, published by Ignite Publishing™, she invites readers on a transformative journey of recognizing the extraordinary within our everyday moments. Diana's personal experiences and insightful reflections effortlessly guide us toward a deeper awareness of the magic that surrounds us—even in the seemingly mundane or less obvious. Expect Magic is more than just a book—it's a gentle reminder that each of us can find beauty, purpose, and meaning in the ordinary, if only we learn to notice it."

—ROBERT STACK
Celebrity Manager and co-author of *Success is a Journey*

"Throughout the pages of Expect Magic, the wise author explores how to awaken and nurture the magic within all of us. I highly recommend this book to all seeking a blueprint for creating your next Encore."

—SUSAN A. MURPHY, PhD.,
Best-selling author of *In the Company of Women, LifeQ, and Leading Successful Teams*

"Diana is a brilliant writer who is both easy to read and enchanting to experience. This book is a legacy of love and leadership that exudes magic in a way that only Diana is capable of. In a world of endless words it seems Diana has mastered something simple and electric that truly stands out as heart-provoking and life changing."

DAVID T. FAGAN
Publicist, Publisher, Producer

"I have personally known Diana for more than 40 years. When people from the outside see her, they are totally awed by her accomplishments and inner and outer beauty. Some think she was born this way with all the advantages that normal people do not have. This is absolutely untrue. I know: I have watched her for decades transform negative situations and challenges into pure gold. She did this through the techniques and mindset described in this book. It's as though she has a direct connection with her Divine Higher Self and shows us how to connect ourselves. Expect Magic is a guide to living an extraordinary life and to having an impact on everyone around you."

—TIM PIERING
Founder of Mastery Circle International,
Martial Arts Master with six black belts, and International Author

"Diana is an inspiring role model for living your truth and taking on life to the fullest. She has a gift for communicating the most profound lessons in a way that lovingly carries you on a magical ride... All I can say is - this book is a must-read!"

– HYLA CASS MD,
Psychiatrist and author of *8 Weeks to Vibrant Health*

Testimonials About Diana

"Diana, I am so happy for your success, your contentment and joy! You are the quintessential essence of a radiant soul!"

— JACK CANFIELD
A Pioneer and legend in the field of personal development and peak performance, founder of the billion-dollar Chicken Soup for the Soul™ publishing empire, Multiple *New York Times* bestselling author.

⸻

"You have inspired me far more over the years than you may know. Diana, you are the epitome of beauty, grace, and spiritual inspiration. You light the path wherever you walk."

—RAMA VERNON, YOGACHARYA
Esteemed yoga teacher known as the "Mother of Yoga in America" and one of the Founders of Yoga Journal. Author of several books.

⸻

"Diana Wentworth is the calmest, most measured, most engaging speaker I've ever heard. Her stories, from dating Elvis Presley in 1959 in Paris to starting the Inside Edge in 1985, are not just mesmerizing but life-changing. Her work with Jack Canfield and Mark Hansen on Chicken Soup for the Soul is equally captivating. Diana's sense of spirituality and the joy of life she exudes are not just inspiring; they're contagious. Don't miss the chance to listen to her speak and to be uplifted by her books!"

—DR. GREG SANDERS
Founder of EZcard

⸻

"Diana has been a dear friend and mentor for me for close to half a century. I don't know anyone with a more positive attitude. From our early days at 'Impact Studios,' to traveling into Russia as 'Citizen Diplomats' in 1985 at the height of the Cold War to four decades of 'Inside Edge' breakfast meetings, Diana has always been the most cheerful, energetic, and transformational leader. Expecting miracles has been key to her life and her legacy."

—TOM SEWELL
Artist and photojournalist, Maui, HI

⸻

"Diana gave the most heartfelt presentation I have ever heard. What a magical life she has lived! A light for all to follow."

—COLIN ROTH
CEO of Speaking Empire

———•————•———

"I can't remember the last time I was moved to tears by a speaker. Diana has a way of touching your heart and inspiring you to do the same for others."

—JENNIFER LONGMORE

———•————•———

"I was inspired by your talk today because it continued my awakening to the hard fact that the movement of the spirit cares not about age or status. It just seeks those open and willing to dream big and act boldly to further humanity. It helps me to see that I, too, walk a path of grace and incredible opportunity. Finally, I found your centering tips quite useful."

— TERRY BRENNAN
Photographer

———•————•———

"Your talk was so loving—so powerful—and I learned some great distinctions. Love your stories!"

—DORIA (DC) CORDOVA
www.MoneyandYou.com

———•————•———

"Diana Wentworth is an enchantress. When she speaks of creating a magical life, she is an embodiment. Her words will make you spellbound in awe of her brilliance."

—JACKIE LAPIN,
Founder of *Speakertunity*, Author of *Practical Conscious Creation:
Daily Techniques to Manifest Your Desires.*

Dedication

To my darling Dr. Lexi Welanetz,

Your radiant spirit heals hearts, especially mine.
Through countless meals and peals of laughter,
you've shown me that wisdom and whimsy make the
perfect blend. Thank you for being both my daughter
and my daily dose of joy.

With infinite love and a dash of mischief, Mom.

Acknowledgment

To my cherished co-author, Lady JB Owen:

Your brilliance illuminated every page of *Expect Magic*. From our first conversation to the final words, your creative spirit and profound understanding of life's magic transformed this book into something far beyond my initial dreams. Through countless hours of collaboration, your wisdom and warmth helped shape not just the words but the very soul of this work. Your partnership has been a gift that turned this book into my most meaningful legacy.

As someone who's spent decades in the publishing world—even reaching the New York Times bestseller list, I thought I knew everything about bringing books to life. But Lady JB Owen showed me something entirely new. I'd been wrestling with writing my twelfth book, *Expect Magic*, for three years, trying to pour all my years of life wisdom into its pages. It was like trying to catch stardust with my bare hands, beautiful but overwhelming. Then JB stepped in, and *oh*, what a transformation!

That's how I discovered someone who doesn't just publish books—she births them. JB has this extraordinary gift of listening with her heart. She hears not just your words but the depth and meaning behind them.

Working with JB was pure joy. She'd sit with me, her eyes sparkling with enthusiasm, and draw out stories I'd forgotten I had. She took my lifetime of experiences, from founding the *Inside Edge Foundation*, which nurtured thought leaders for 39 years, to all my adventures in between and helped me weave them into something beautiful.

What makes JB truly special? It's her rare combination of wisdom and spontaneity, perception and playfulness. She doesn't just help you write a book; she helps you reveal your heart's truth in ways that dance off the page.

If you're looking for a creative partner who will cherish your story as much as you do, JB Owen isn't just the best choice; she's a gift to the writing world. She's not just my publisher; she's a treasured colleague who helped me make my magic accessible to you.

Thank you, dear friend, for believing so deeply in our vision and for weaving your own magical thread through every chapter. Sharing this journey of discovery with you has made it all the more joyful.

With profound gratitude and love,

Diana von Welanetz Wentworth

Contents

xv

Foreword By
Lady JB Owen

There are only a few times in life when you realize the *magic* of a moment as it unfolds. More often, we look back and reflect on something special or reminisce about a situation that grew to be something magical. The moment I met Diana was *magic* occurring within itself. We connected on a Zoom™ call, and from the second her stunning smile appeared on the screen, I was captivated. For the next hour, we spoke about music, relationships, spirituality, writing, traveling, and the art of life itself. We giddily conversed like two girls who had known each other for decades and immediately settled into ourselves like two souls who had ventured together for eons. Diana's ease and grace brought forth my own comfort. Her effervescence

1

was contagious, and the way she spoke about essence and existence encouraged me to speak the same. I remember distinctly thinking about how she was outwardly beautiful and inwardly radiant. Her zest for life and reverence for humanity formed an instant connection, and like *magic,* we were new, lifelong friends.

Like most friendships forged in a cosmic coming together, Diana and I learned many things from each other. We conversed about business, books, and marketing. We chatted about the state of the world, the changing of the times, and the importance of human consciousness. She showed me that there are magical gifts in times of struggle or hardship. She emphasized that when we ask, we receive, allowing the Universe to work its *magic* in our favor. Through many hours of discussions and contemplations, she deeply impacted me with the knowledge that, when we expect it, *magic* comes eagerly into our lives. It's woven into the fabric of every day: always present, always available.

I have always felt *magic* surrounding my life, and my many conversations with Diana reminded me of when I was very young, going to Sunday school and hearing how God wanted me to have *everything.* He was just waiting to give me all the gifts in the world. I was told of a magical room filled with a mountain of presents, all ready and waiting for me to open. God had an endless supply of treasures waiting for me to unwrap. All I had to do was be willing to open them and see what *magic* was inside.

Armed with this information, I have gone about my life believing that His gifts are always present, magically wanting to come into my life, divinely waiting to be utilized, and wondrously excited to show up. I anticipate, trust, and expect these *presents*. When I step into their *presence* and know they are there for me, they magically come into my life.

Diana and I often spoke of this synergistic understanding that such *magic* is fostered by *believing* it exists. We reflected on how many people in today's day and age have forgotten, forsaken, or even rejected the idea that such *magic* is ever present. Many people have lost their connection to the blessings of *magic,* just waiting to blossom in their lives. They have succumbed to the scrutiny and comparisons, allowing what *is* to determine what could *be*.

Amidst countless conversations about the topics of *magic*, divinity, God, consciousness, and beliefs, Diana and I agreed that people need to be reminded that the *magic* of the Universe is at their very fingertips. And the ability to call it into existence is part of their birthright, a gift given for them to enjoy. Diana felt that, in her life, she had experienced *magic* countless times. I agree that m*agic* is all around us and living through us when we decide not just to imagine it but expect it to come into being.

Our love for the topic of intentional and intended *magic* forged a commonality between us that created several serendipitous moments, delightful encounters, and beloved memories. Diana became a guide, weaving me through the possibilities, opportunities, and blessings that came because of our love and understanding of what *magic* means. We found deeper laughter, richer conversations, and more purpose in the way we lived.

I took notice when Diana spoke about how *magic* had not just influenced her life but defined her trajectory. When she shared delightful encounters or better-than-she-could-have-imagined outcomes, I listened. When much of what she had learned in her eighty years of living centered around the *magic* she believed existed in her life, I wanted to know how such *magic* could be harnessed, cultivated, and further experienced.

There are moments in life when we know, deep within, that we're being called to do something meaningful and extraordinary, even if we can't fully explain it. One such moment came on a beautiful day in July when Diana and I decided it was time to capture her lifetime of magical experiences and share them with the world. Our idea wasn't just about writing a book; it was about distilling her wisdom, stories, and insights into a living guide for others to discover the *magic* waiting to unfold in their lives.

With her dictating heartfelt reflections and me eagerly taking copious notes, we began crafting the essence of 'expecting' *magic*. Diana poured into me her understanding of how to create *magic* and, more importantly, how to envision it with unwavering intention. She shared the essential ingredients of patience, trust, and joy that fuel the m*agic* we seek. She outlined the processes and practices that awaken this extraordinary force, detailing how frequency and consistency can turn simple moments into miraculous ones. She held nothing back, unveiling her lifelong discoveries with generosity and grace.

Working with Diana has been one of the most meaningful experiences of my life. Through her stories, I witnessed the undeniable power of expecting *magic* to create life's sublime enchantments. Through my artistry with words, I've had the privilege of weaving her wisdom into these pages and capturing just how she defines *magic* as a power we all possess. The process of bringing this book to life has felt sacred—a shared journey of connection, creativity, and purpose. I know that *magic* was at work to bring us together and produce this book for *you*.

After months of refining and hours of back and forth, *Expect Magic* came to life as a guide to help spark the awareness of what is possible in everyone's life. The effort and long hours Diana and I put into it were worth it, as each page has become a beacon of what can happen when we believe and *Expect Magic* in our lives. The ideas, suggestions, and tools in the book are designed to arouse the *magic* in you, to share the room full of many presents, and to make the mountain of gifts available yours to open and experience magnificently.

As you journey through these chapters, you will feel that spark of *magic* igniting within you, and you will be inspired to receive life's gifts with a renewed sense of wonder and joy, knowing that *magic* is already surrounding you, just waiting to be embraced.

Diana's gentle encouragement has awakened something profound within me and now within you—a deeper understanding of how joy and gratitude attract synchronicity and how *magic* is always at work when we believe in it. She has been a gift in my life, showing me how the smallest moments can open grand doors and how our presence, imbued with love and intention, can transform humanity.

I will forever be grateful for Diana's luminous presence and boundless wisdom, and it's an honor to share this magical journey with her—and now, with you. This book is an invitation to awaken your own *magic* and step into a life filled with wonder, joy, and infinite possibility. *Magic* is here, ready to be received. All you have to do is welcome it in!

With love and blessings,

Lady JB Owen

Preface

There comes a time in every person's life when they want to do more than just share; they want to *impact*, *awaken*, and *inspire* in a greater way. This usually happens at a pivotal moment in their life when something monumental has occurred, or they have reached a certain age or chapter in their life that reminds them of how much they have learned and what they have within them that they can give back to the world.

Having made circles around the sun for over eighty years, I've learned a tremendous amount, experienced *many* lessons, felt the reverberation of significant moments, and sensed within me a *deep* desire to give *more* so that others can enjoy a richer understanding within themselves. This quest to give and share more comes at a time when the world is changing rapidly, and life often feels more complicated than ever before. It seems we all need greater guidance to navigate what the future holds, and many of us are asking bigger questions with the answers yet to be discovered.

At this stage in my life, I have witnessed many changes in society, technology, and thought. I have seen people, communities, and families evolve, and I have observed the interactions of individuals in business, recreation, and commerce expand and stretch to their very limits. I have watched the world change dramatically, and I have often been at the forefront of emerging trends and alternative ways of thinking. I can happily say I have danced the Bop and the Twist, stood on the stages of advocacy, traveled to Russia during the Cold War, become a *New York Times* best-selling author, and formed the premier group of transformational thought leaders on the cusp of self-development. I have been a part of both the 'growing' trends and what some might consider 'controversial' ideas. All of which have led me here to this moment, sharing what I have learned with you.

Pushing the boundaries toward learning and discovering *more* has always been a part of my genetic makeup and is in every fiber of my Being. I didn't just want to live; I wanted to live life to the fullest. I wanted to feel all the emotions and experience all the possibilities that came with life: marriage, parenting, entrepreneurship, and thought leadership. Today, I can confidently say I accomplished huge successes, enjoyed glorious moments, passed through innumerable dark nights of the soul, endured heart-breaking losses, and felt life's glorious kaleidoscope of emotions to the fullest by challenging myself to live fearlessly.

Many have looked upon my life and asked me how I did it. *How did I go on dates with Elvis Presley, host a successful TV show, marry two amazing husbands, and be a part of a franchise that sold over 500 million books?* They want to know how I have connected with the most dynamic people, found the perfect home, created lifelong friendships, and put myself in situations that always seemed to work out. Many have looked at my life and the work I have done to make a difference, inspiring and advocating for those less fortunate, and in seeing the positive outcome it has created, they ask me, "How do you do it? What's the trick?"

Living life to the fullest is not a trick, nor is it luck or happenstance. To live the best of what the world offers, one must be willing to welcome, play, and dance with the essence of *magic itself*. Yes, that magical force we each possess within. *Magic* is the key ingredient to all that one can enjoy, all we receive, and all we desire to give back. *Magic*, in its amazing force, has been with me every step of my life. It's been both my best friend and my secret ingredient. It has shown up when I least expected it and when I needed it most. *Magic* has been not just the key but the crucial component to making the most out of life and experiencing the magnificence of one's soul.

I have come to understand that *magic* is that profound force that fuels our dreams and aspirations. It nudges us to look beyond the ordinary and invites us to trust in possibilities that seem beyond our reach. *Magic* is the spark that awakens our passions and compels us to *pursue our dreams*. It is a whisper in the wind, a trusted feeling, and a gentle nudge that propels us forward. *Magic* is the force *within* our knowing heart, and by using the power of that magic, we can continually astonish ourselves on our journey by accomplishing wonders.

At this pinnacle stage in my life, as I reflect on the remarkable moments that have shaped my existence, I realize that *magic* has been present not only in grand experiences but also in everyday miracles. It is in the connections I have forged with others, the love I have both given and received, and amidst all the simple joys that fill my days and offer meaning. Knowing that such a force has been instrumental in my life, I believe that speaking about expecting *magic* and sharing it will expand its abilities and invite more of it into other people's lives.

This book is my invitation to invite and *Expect Magic* in your life. It is my way of pulling back the curtain to show that you, too, can live a life filled with purpose, wonder, and boundless effervescence. Since *magic* has the ability to create positive change and leave a lasting impact, let this be your guide to recognizing and nurturing the magic that resides in you. Open your heart to the unseen forces that *magic* brings. Weave it throughout your experiences, allowing it to guide you toward a future filled with all that wants to come into existence to support you.

As you turn the page and read this book, I invite you to find inspiration, follow your heart, pursue your passions, and create a life filled with endless *magic* designed Divinely just *for* you. When you decide to *Expect Magic*, I guarantee it *will* wondrously arrive.

With a gracious heart,

Diana von Welanetz Wentworth

Expect
Magic

The Power of Expectation

Imagine, if you will, the exciting and delightful feeling of every day being filled with *magic. Wouldn't it be marvelous to wake each morning with the notion that something profound, wondrous, and extraordinary was about to unfold? How different would your life be if the swirl of magic surrounded all you envisioned and made it not only possible but destined?*

I'd like you to suspend all other beliefs for a moment and envision how your life would be if you could completely trust the serendipity, amazement, and *magic* of creating what you desire. If you were to shift your entire thinking to *Expect Magic*, knowing it would arrive, *what magic would you be enthused to materialize?*

Most people do not ask themselves such questions. They feel stuck in the mundane and bound by their circumstances. So many feel lost, and their hope for *magic* has vanished. They have succumbed to its absence or even shunned its presence. Forsaking their desires, they stick to living life as it is 'supposed to be.'

From a young age, I felt an empowering whisper within me, a call to welcome something beyond the ordinary, to trust a powerful force that I could sense lived within me. Life's mundane routines and societal expectations often served to mute that whisper. *Still, the desire persisted*, guiding me on a path of transforming my life so that I could become a 'shining mirror' to others in transforming theirs.

Such a process hasn't been a smooth one. I've faced obstacles that seemed insurmountable, times of darkness, and moments of despair that threatened to make me lose heart. But through it all, I have learned to *Expect Magic* to be on my side. Expecting *magic* isn't about conjuring up a perfect life; *it's about developing an ever-growing determination to find the extraordinary in the midst of the ordinary. It's about transforming pain into purpose and struggles into steppingstones.* I deeply know that all that unfolds has a reason, and it is how we hold it in our minds that makes all the difference.

This book is a testament to the journey of discovering one's innate *magic*, a journey that will reveal the incredible power of expectation. How expecting something to materialize gives it the energy it requires to *come into Being.* Expecting *magic* isn't about ignoring the challenges and hardships of life; it's about embracing them with an unwavering belief that obstacles are opportunities and that *something wondrous awaits around the corner.* It's about evoking positive expectations and allowing the Universe to provide uninhibited. When we *Expect Magic*, we invite more into our lives, encouraging what we desire to show up in uniquely unexpected ways.

Expecting *magic* begins with a shift in mindset. It starts with discovering and cultivating a knowing that you are worthy of the extraordinary and that the Universe is conspiring in your favor. It's about setting positive intentions and opening your heart to the infinite possibilities that lie ahead.

In the following pages, I will share the lessons I've learned, along with the practices that have transformed my life and stories that have inspired me to *keep cultivating my belief in the power of magic.* Each chapter is designed to guide you through many aspects of this transformative way of thinking and shows you how, by living in a state of joy and embracing change with anticipation and expectation, you will connect with and magnify the essence of the *magic* that *lives within you.*

As you embark on this exploration, I encourage you to have an open mind and receiving heart. Let go of any preconceived notions or limiting beliefs that distract you. Embrace the power of *magic* with a sense of curiosity and an emerging sense of awe. Let what you are about to learn be the beginning of the life *you are meant to enjoy.* Trust that you are exactly where you need to be and that every experience, no matter how it appears or unfolds, is a part of your magical journey toward your Divine destiny.

I encourage you to explore the power of expectation and the *magic* that unfolds when you dare to trust. As you embark on the process of transformation and discover the incredible power that lies within the *magic* you are about to access, embody that excitement. If you are willing to trust in exploring the extraordinary and be one of the few who *know there is more*, you *will* invoke the *magic* within you to create a life of wonder, meaning, and purpose that will light up your life and the lives of so many more.

Your journey to *Expect Magic* is ready to begin.

Magic is in all of Us

WHAT *MAGIC* IS

In a world overflowing with practical advice and logical strategies for achieving success, you might wonder why I suggest turning your attention to something as seemingly intangible as *magic*. The word "*magic*" might evoke images of illusions or impossible feats, things hard to believe or explain. But for those of us willing to embrace it, *magic* represents the profound, invisible forces that guide our lives toward harmony, wonder, and alignment with our highest good.

To me, *magic* isn't about pulling rabbits out of hats or using a sleight of hand. It's about the quiet miracles, the Divine synchronicities, and the awe-inspiring moments that seem to arrive just when we need them most. *Magic* is the inexplicable alignment of circumstances that guide us into clarity, ease, and joy. It whispers to us through unexpected opportunities, meaningful coincidences, and timely insights, urging us to trust in the Universe's infinite wisdom.

Magic is always available, always surrounding us. It's the thread connecting us to the energy of the cosmos, the unseen rhythm of life that beats for our highest good. When we learn to *Expect Magic*, we invite a partnership with this energy. Suddenly, what once felt difficult begins to flow, and what seemed out of reach becomes possible. Expecting *magic* is not wishful thinking; it's a profound practice of believing in and leaning into the interconnectedness of all things.

For many of us, the idea of *magic* seems whimsical, even naïve. We're taught to value hard work, logic, and tangible results. And while these are important, they don't tell the whole story. Life is not just a series of steps and strategies; it's a dance of energy, intuition, and possibility. *Magic* is the unseen partner in this dance, leading us toward experiences and outcomes beyond anything we could plan or predict.

When we open ourselves to *magic*, we move beyond the limitations of what we think is possible. We step into a realm where creativity flourishes, where solutions appear out of nowhere, and where life feels richer, more vibrant, and more meaningful. *Magic* doesn't replace effort; it amplifies it. It's the invisible force that lifts you, guiding you to soar toward horizons you once thought were beyond your reach.

WHERE MY *MAGIC* BEGAN

When I was a young child, I often felt withdrawn after a terrible bout with my father, who struggled to control his anger. His temper left me speechless, closed off, judging myself as a failure and worn down with unworthiness. At the same time, I felt confused about why he wanted to live that way. *Why did he allow anger to consume his daily life?* Even at a young age, I knew there had to be a better choice and that life could be filled with joy and contentment. I knew that I preferred to live with grace and happiness.

It was at this young age I encountered *magic* for the first time in a way that would shape the rest of my life. After a horribly upsetting encounter with my father, I sat alone on my bed, feeling lost and unworthy. Suddenly, I heard a voice—a calm, reassuring presence that said, "Nothing really bad will ever happen to you." Though I was alone, the voice filled the room with warmth and comfort, as if an unseen presence were wrapping me in its embrace.

That moment was pure *magic*. It wasn't just the words; it was the knowing they carried. It felt as though life itself had reached out to tell me I was safe, loved, and held. From that day forward, I understood that *magic* wasn't something external or far away; it was *within* me, a force I could turn to for guidance, comfort, and inspiration.

Over time, I began to *Expect Magic*. I didn't need to force it or search for it; I simply believed it was there. And because I believed, it showed up—in moments of doubt, in times of hardship, and in everyday joys. When challenges arose, *magic* reminded me that solutions were always near. When the path ahead felt unclear, *magic* lit the way.

Looking back, I see that my belief in *magic* wasn't just a passive hope; it was an active force that shaped my reality. My expectation was like an open door, inviting the Universe to step in and surprise me. And time after time, it did.

Truthfully, my journey in life has not been perfect, and I have faced many of the same hardships and setbacks we all encounter. Yet, at 83 years old, I recognize that experiencing and expecting *magic* gave *magic* the fuel it needed to be a constant feature in my life. My belief that *magic* was there brought it into being. The deep knowing I had inside that there was an inner power to support me made people, solutions, new ideas, and opportunities effortlessly appear. It was through my *expectation* that *magic* materialized.

MAGIC AND YOU

I believe that you have picked up this book because, on some level, you believe—or want to believe—that *magic* is a marvelous force and that it can transform your life. Maybe you're at a point where you're ready for something new, something wondrous, something extraordinary. Or perhaps you've had glimpses of *magic* before and are eager to invite more of it into your life.

As you begin this journey, I want you to know that *magic* is already with you. It's not something you need to earn or deserve; it's your birthright. From the moment you took your first breath, *magic* has been woven into the fabric of your being. It whispers to you in moments of stillness, nudges you toward unexpected opportunities, and wraps itself around you in times of need. All you have to do is *expect* it.

When you approach life with an open heart and a sense of wonder, you create the perfect conditions for *magic* to appear. This openness is an invitation, a signal to the Universe that you're ready to receive its gifts. It's about seeing the world not just as it is but as it could be, filled with infinite possibilities and hidden treasures waiting to be discovered. With each curious question you ask, each hopeful thought you hold, and each courageous step you take, you amplify the energy of *magic* in your life.

Expecting *magic* invites you to pay attention to the connections and coincidences that hint at a bigger picture. It's about leaning into gratitude for the small joys, knowing they're part of a much larger masterpiece. Even the obstacles along your journey hold their own kind of *magic*, offering lessons and redirection toward paths you might not have otherwise discovered.

To *Expect Magic* is to live with a sense of playful openness. It means being willing to say "yes" to possibilities, even when they don't come wrapped in the way you expect. It's about showing up for life with a hopeful spirit, trusting that each step you take is guided and that the journey itself is infused with wonder and purpose.

MAKING THE MOST OF THIS BOOK

I want you to imagine, right now, what it would feel like to live a life filled with *magic*. Picture the ease, the joy, and the wonder of knowing that an infinite, loving force supports you. Imagine the synchronicities, the meaningful encounters, and the delightful surprises that await you. The moment you begin to seek *magic* is the moment you discover it.

Bringing *magic* into your life isn't about adding one more thing to your to-do list. It's about shifting your perspective, opening your heart, and embracing the excitement of what's possible. As you begin to *Expect Magic*, you'll notice it everywhere—in small moments of beauty, in unexpected opportunities, and in the quiet whispers of your intuition.

As you move through the pages of this book, let yourself be curious, open, and playful. Suspend any doubts or skepticism, and simply allow yourself to explore. *Magic* doesn't need you to believe in it; it only needs you to be willing to see it. Therefore, use practices, insights, and stories I share to help you recognize and cultivate *magic* in your life. See where *magic* has already shown up, invite more of it intentionally, and trust in its power to guide you faithfully.

As you read each chapter, you'll discover how to bring *magic* into your life. Over the years, I have synthesized how to awaken its wonder by using *magic* myself. Through personal stories, antidotes, and mindset shifts, I reveal how *magic* can be activated. I show you how you can use your gifts and abilities to fuel the *magic* you possess. As you dive into the teachings, reflect on your thoughts and find ways to expand any limitations. Allow the ideas to permeate your thinking and influence your actions. As the days progress, explore where you can use what I have shared to bring more *magic* forth. Allow each idea to be a seed germinating, a dream materializing, and a way of being that fortifies your existence. *Magic* is everywhere; you just have to be shown how to harness it, and each chapter does just that.

The journey ahead is one of discovery, transformation, and joy. I promise that if you open your heart to *magic*, it will meet you halfway. It will show up in ways that surprise and delight you and guide you toward a life that feels deeply aligned with your true self.

As you take this step forward, embrace the *magic* that's waiting for you. See where it leads. Welcome its gifts. This is going to be fun, exciting, and full of wonder because when we expect it, *magic* arrives.

Magic is in each of us. What you are about to learn from this page onward is the key to unleashing the *magic* that resides inside of you!

"Those who don't believe in magic will never find it."

—ROALD DAHL

Chapter 1

Living in a State of Joy

Every moment holds the potential to awaken something extraordinary. The essence of *magic* isn't bound to fairy tales or distant dreams; it's woven into the fabric of our daily lives, waiting for us to notice, invite, and ignite it. *Magic* begins with intention, with an openness to something greater than ourselves.

We all know the genie emerges when you summon it by rubbing the lamp. Friction between two sticks sparks a flame. Pressure on a grain of sand transforms it into a pearl. Pulling back an arrow propels it forward, and shaping clay allows it to take form. Just as every creation has a catalyst, something must occur to awaken *magic* and bring it to life.

It isn't enough to wish for *magic*; it must be sparked. Just as a flame is born from friction, the energy to awaken *magic* resides in our willingness to create, align, and embrace the extraordinary. After years of aligning myself with the power of *magic*, I have come to know that the key to all *magic* lies in the vibrations we exude, and the most powerful of all those vibrations is the vibration of internal *JOY*.

Many paths can lead to welcoming *magic* into your life. Still, the simplest and most transformative way to begin accessing your *magic* is by mastering the art of *cultivating* and *embodying joy*. Joy is not just an emotion but a powerful, magnetic energy. When we choose joy and generate it from within, it creates a high vibration that becomes the fertile ground for *magic* to flourish. Joyful energy fuels the *magic* we seek and invites it to ripple outward, transforming our experiences and touching everything around us.

Joy is believed to radiate at one of the highest vibrational frequencies, measured on the Hertz scale at approximately 540 Hz. This frequency represents a state of expansive energy, where our minds feel elevated, our hearts open, and our spirits align with a profound sense of well-being.

Everything in the Universe is energy, vibrating at different frequencies, and this includes our emotions and thoughts. The concept of vibrational frequency suggests that the energy we emit influences what we attract and experience. Higher frequencies such as love (528 Hz), joy (540 Hz), and gratitude (around 540 Hz) resonate with states of harmony and abundance, while lower frequencies such as fear (100 Hz) and anger (150 Hz) correspond to emotions that can create discord and stagnation.

Joy is one of the very highest energy frequencies that humans can experience. That means when you are joyful, your body and mind vibrate at a high frequency, producing a sense of lightness, openness, and positivity that *magic* adores. You feel more optimistic, capable, and energized when you vibrate at a higher frequency. It's like tuning into a radio station that plays uplifting music; everything around you seems brighter and more enjoyable. At this frequency, your heart is more open to giving and receiving. You become more empathetic and connected, which enhances your relationships and interactions with the world.

Vibrating at a frequency of joy serves as a power source of *magic*. It is the force that *magic* needs to perform its wondrous tasks and support your dreams. With the energy of joy, *magic* awakens like a sleeping dragon filled with power and velocity. It is like the gas in the car, the match to the wick, and the plutonium to the rocket ship.

Joy activates *magic* and gives it life. Joy inspires *magic* to formulate itself into its wondrous existence.

If you've been wondering where *magic* is in your life, it's time to ask yourself an important question: *How much joy are you truly experiencing?* Joy isn't just a fleeting feeling or a temporary high; it's a powerful, magnetic force that shapes your reality and invites *magic* to unfold. When you allow yourself to bask in genuine joy, you naturally attract positive experiences, meaningful opportunities, and inspiring people who resonate with your energy. The more you choose joy, the more you amplify your ability to recognize the extraordinary in the everyday. Joy isn't just the key to inviting *magic* into your life; it's the energy that makes it inevitable.

Take a moment right now to ask yourself: *Are you giving joy the space it deserves? Are you welcoming joy in your life, participating in joy-filled actions, and embodying joy in your attitude? Are you choosing joy over other lower vibrational states? Is there joy in your life?* Answering these key questions will be the foundation as we go forward.

I can attest that by tuning into the vibrant frequency of joy, you become an active participant in the *magic* that is always waiting to manifest. Envision joy as a luminous magnet, radiating outwards and pulling in all the elements that align with your highest self.

JOY CREATES *MAGIC*

When I was three years old, I met Alice Blair in a Divine encounter and perfectly aligned coincidence, and she became my joy-filled guide and endearing best friend. Alice lived in a constant state of joy. I watched her throughout my school years be the epitome of joy. From the moment she stuck up for me in grade two to our grade twelve graduation and prom, Alice exuded joy and proved that from a place of joyful emotions, magic always showed up.

Alice wasn't what society considered the prettiest or what schools labeled as the smartest, but she was a master at being kind, open, warm, and joyous. She radiated happiness and always found the glass not just half-full but overflowing in every circumstance. Her sense of goodness far exceeded the silly things others were obsessed with, and for Alice, the lemons life delivered were both juicy and sweet. She preferred grace, acceptance, and patience and always believed that everything worked out better with a dash of joy-filled expectation.

When I was growing up, I lived in a very challenging household. Things were not happy or at peace in our home; when my life was struggling or I felt depressed, Alice would remind me of the joy that lived around every corner and that rainbows are always found at the end of a rainstorm. She was the person who proved that magical experiences come from the frequency of joy. She taught me that ser-endipitous delight, beautiful encounters, possibilities beyond beliefs, and glorious heart-pounding moments are all a product of the joy we generate. Her life was not perfect, and she faced her share of tests, but through her, I witnessed how joy fixes everything. It changes destinies, moves us through obstacles, opens hearts, expands the mind, and with undaunting faith, fulfills our dreams.

I owe so much to Alice, who, during those pivotal years when worry and self-doubt could have taken hold, showed me the power of joy. She helped me see that joy was more than an emotion; it was a way of being. I began to weave it into my conversations, anchor it in my heart, and release the burdens of negativity that no longer served me. Joy became my true north, a compass guiding me toward a life brim-ming with possibility. Under joy's guidance, I watched *magic* awaken and flow into my life in unexpected and profoundly beautiful ways.

JOY AS A COMPASS

Now it is time for you to imagine navigating life with joy as your compass, guiding your every decision. When we use joy as our North Star, we align ourselves with our true selves and highest purpose. Making choices that bring about genuine joy allows us to live authentically and let our innermost yearnings shape our journey. Joy is a powerful indicator of where our soul wants to go and what we can attract.

Living in a state of joy allows us to move through life with ease and authenticity, not out of force or obligation but in alignment with our true selves. When we embrace joy, opportunities naturally reveal themselves, guiding us like a beacon toward our highest potential.

In her book *Finding Your Own North Star*, author Martha Beck beautifully illustrates this concept. She writes about discovering one's True North, a metaphor for finding our authentic self and aligning with it in all aspects of life. This focused direction is precisely what using joy as a compass entails: having clarity and direction toward manifesting what matters most.

When I became open and receptive to my highest good, I moved into a state of expectancy and joyful openness. Changing my life's course became effortless as I was guided by what joyfully lit me up. Life turned to trusting joy to lead the way, knowing it would never steer me wrong or make life complicated. By focusing on what joy could accomplish, I enhanced my experiences and ultimately radiated positivity back into the world and to those around me.

HOW TO ACHIEVE A STATE OF JOY

To begin your journey of expecting *magic*, let *joy* be your true north. Each morning, as you awaken, ask yourself, "Where is the most joy to be found today?" Repeat this inquiry throughout your day, inviting joy to guide your actions and decisions. Trust its influence, knowing that joy illuminates the path toward your highest good.

Living in a state of joy means actively choosing to see the world through a joyful lens. Joy is not merely a way to feel but a profound state of being, a way to transform ordinary moments into extraordinary experiences. When we embrace joy, we unlock a realm where normality becomes miraculous, and new possibilities unfold effortlessly.

By aligning with joy, you set the stage for *magic* to manifest. Opportunities become clearer, relationships deepen, and challenges begin to ease. Joy is the compass that always points you in the right direction, guiding you toward experiences that resonate with your truest self.

As you welcome joy into your daily life, watch how it transforms your perspective and the world around you. The energy of joy is magnetic; it attracts more of what uplifts, inspires, and aligns with your highest potential. In choosing joy, you create a life that brims with wonder, beauty, and *magic* that wants to unfold.

If you have forgotten how to create joy or did not learn how to bring about joy, here are some powerful ways to manifest more joy and, in turn, more *magic* in all your activities.

JOY MANIFESTING PRACTICES

Practice Gratitude:
- Manifesting joy doesn't require grand gestures or monumental changes; it begins with simple moments of appreciation. By acknowledging the blessings in our lives, no matter how small, we shift our focus from what we lack to what we have. This shift in perspective is like planting seeds in a garden. As we nurture these seeds with appreciation, they bloom into an abundant harvest.
- Focus on the positive aspects of your life and express gratitude for them. This simple practice will elevate your frequency and attract more joyful experiences.

Engage in Activities You Love:
- Whether dancing, painting, sharing tea with others, or spending time in nature, engage in activities that bring you genuine pleasure. These moments of joy will naturally raise your vibrational frequency.
- A proven way to cultivate joy is through mindfulness of presence. When we immerse ourselves fully in the present moment,

we free ourselves from the burdens of the past and the anxieties of the future. We discover the *magic* that exists in the here and now—the laughter of a child, the beauty of a sunset, the warmth of a loved one's embrace. Each moment becomes an invitation to experience life in its purest, most joyful form.

Surround Yourself with Positive People:

- Being around uplifting and inspiring people can significantly impact your energy frequency. Their positivity boosts your mood and helps maintain a state of joy.

- Imagine a world where everyone embraces joy as a way of life. It would be a world filled with compassion, empathy, and connection, where differences are celebrated and love reigns supreme. As we cultivate joy within ourselves, we contribute to creating positivity, one moment at a time.

- Perhaps the most beautiful aspect of living in a state of joy is its ripple effect. Joy is contagious; we spark others when we radiate it. Our joy becomes a beacon, illuminating the paths of those we encounter and inviting them to join us on this journey of magic and wonder.

Finding Joy in the Journey:

- Living in a state of joy involves letting go of any need for perfection. It means enjoying the journey rather than fixating on the destination. When we choose to savor each step along the path, we open our hearts to a myriad of joyful experiences we might easily miss.

- To live joyfully is to cultivate resilience. It's about acknowledging that life is a series of ups and downs; through it all, we can remain rooted in joy. This doesn't mean ignoring pain or hardship but finding strength to rise above them, knowing that joy is within reach.

When you live in a state of joy, you align yourself with infinite possibilities. It's as if you are tapping into a Universal current that invites *magic* to flow effortlessly into your life. Living in a state of joy is a choice. By embracing joy, we become co-creators with the mystery of the Universe, weaving a tapestry of wonder and delight that enriches our lives and the lives of others.

Magic is not complicated nor out of reach. By embracing joy as a way of life, you illuminate your path with love, laughter, and light, the many ingredients of *magic*. You, in turn, give *magic* permission to guide you and produce untold treasures. Since you determine your state and define your frequency, I hope you will dance with the rhythm of the Divine, knowing that the key to a magical life lies *within* the joy *you* create.

"Scatter joy!"

—RALPH WALDO EMERSON

Chapter 2

Shifting from Ego to Essence

There comes a time in every person's life when we must decide whether to keep chasing our ego's desires or embrace our true essence—the deepest, most authentic part of who we are. For many of us, this shift isn't a grand revelation but a gradual journey of self-discovery inspired by the experiences that shape our lives. In this chapter, I want to share my journey of moving from ego to essence, finding my center amidst the chaos, and aligning with the purpose that resonates at the core of my being so that you, too, can find this place in your life, centeredness that comes from being a place of essence and peace versus ego and *edging goodness out*.

As a young girl, I was keenly aware of the expectations and desires projected onto me by society, particularly around appearance and success. This awareness became even more pronounced when, in the midst of an exceedingly awkward puberty, I attended modeling school. There, I learned to walk a certain way, smile just right, and present myself according to beauty standards imposed upon me. I became increasingly conscious of how my mother, grandmother, our community, and society felt about fashion and social status. I found myself caught in a quagmire of striving to meet those constant expectations while honoring what I valued about myself.

The desire to be accepted by the world, to fit in and be admired, fueled my young ego. I remember being obsessed with my looks, constantly checking the mirror to ensure my appearance was acceptable. The modeling school taught me how to present myself to the world, but it also made me acutely aware of the judgment that came with every misstep or flaw. I felt an intense pressure to be perfect, to look perfect, and to live up to an image that was only the surface of me.

As a teen, I began associating my worth with my appearance and how others perceived me. The compliments I received boosted my ego and temporarily filled the void of my insecurities. Yet, the focus on external validation also made me feel hollow and disconnected from my true self. I was striving to fit into a mold that society had created, not realizing that in doing so, I was losing touch with who I genuinely was.

Looking back, I realize how our egos become interwoven with the superficial pursuit of looks and status. The more one chases after these things, the more distant we become from our essence. Living in a state of constant comparison, I was always measuring myself against others and feeling inadequate when I didn't measure up. My ego became a shield, protecting me from the fear of not being enough, but it also kept me from experiencing the deeper connections and true joy that come from living authentically.

EGO VS. ESSENCE

I've learned that ego is often about striving—striving to be seen, to achieve, and to control. It's driven by fear and the need for external validation. Essence, however, draws in *magic*. It's a quieter, more powerful force that doesn't need to shout to be heard. It attracts rather than demands, aligning us with our true purpose and the unique gifts we may offer the world. My friend Gary Zukav, author of *Seat of the Soul,* refers to this awareness as "aligning the personality with the soul."

While ego might scream for attention, essence whispers, inviting us to listen, to slow down, and to connect with what truly matters. Much of my teaching over the years has shown people how to move from an egoic existence to a balanced state of being and a homecoming to one's authentic self. I now use a set of reminders that help me return to my essence whenever I feel scattered or lost. One simple practice is placing my hand on my heart, a reminder to come home to myself whenever I notice I am acting out of ego. My heart is my home base, my place of peace and centeredness. Making the hand-heart connection reinforces my knowing that my heart is the source of my power, not the intensity of my ego.

I have used this technique so effectively that I developed a whole book around it: *Love Your Heart: Follow the Red Thread to a Heart-Centered Life.* The title is based on an ancient archetype of human consciousness. In traditions and cultures around the world, a red thread, rope, or string is a metaphor for love and connection. An ancient Chinese proverb relates that an invisible red thread connects those who are destined to meet. It is said the thread may stretch or tangle but will never break regardless of circumstances. In Inuit culture, the red thread weaves together the tapestry of meaning in our lives.

My passion for heart-centeredness started as a campaign I created when I became a spokeswoman for the American Heart Association following my first heart attack in 2009. I followed a deep desire to write a book to be given out at *Go Red for Women* luncheons that encouraged care of not only the physical heart but also the emotional and spiritual heart. The red thread is the perfect symbol of our inner and outer connectedness, for our hearts sit at the very intersection of our body and our soul. Through our veins and capillaries, the red thread of blood connects our physical heart with every other part of our body, and the ineffable red thread of lore connects our emotional heart, the center of our feelings of well-being, with the spiritual thread of similarity and connection with every other living being.

The book grew into a free resource that many have found helpful. One technique involves placing your hand on your heart, breathing deeply, and feeling who you are at your core. This simple practice can help you reconnect with your essence and navigate life's challenges from a place of love and self-care. If you'd like to access and download this valuable, heart-centered resource, visit my website, www.DianaWentworth.com

In addition to loving your heart, mindful breathing is another simple yet profound practice that helps me step out of the ego and reconnect with my essence. Whenever you feel overwhelmed by the day's demands or caught up in comparison and judgment, take a moment to focus on your breath. Close your eyes and take a deep breath through your nose, feeling your lungs expand. Hold for a moment, then exhale slowly through your mouth, releasing any tension or stress.

As you continue to breathe mindfully, let go of thoughts that do not serve you. Imagine each breath in as drawing in peace and clarity and each breath out as releasing fear and ego-driven concerns. By focusing on long exhales of your breath, you bring yourself back to the present, where your true self resides. This practice costs nothing but offers you everything: calmness, presence, and a deeper connection to your authentic self.

Integrating these simple, no-cost practices into your daily routine allows you to shift from an ego-driven mindset to living from essence. It's in these small, consistent actions that true transformation happens.

FROM SURVIVING TO THRIVING

For many of us, our egos stem from a place of survival. This part of us has been shaped by fears, insecurities, and the need to fit in or be accepted. For me, the wounds from childhood bullying and the pressure to conform led me to develop a defense mechanism that was deeply ego-driven. I became obsessed with looking good and gaining approval, a common trap many of us fall into.

But life's greatest teachers, those who embody their essence, remind us that we are capable of much more. I was fortunate to have such people in my life, guiding me back to my true self whenever I strayed too far from my path. One of those people was my brother, Eugene Webb. He was a profound example of living from essence rather than ego. He was the embodiment of a true role model in many ways, especially for someone like me who was seeking to move beyond superficial desires. Gino was always more interested in seeking truth and honoring the more meaningful aspects of life. His centered and soulful outlook on life gave me a comprehensive understanding of more expansive paths that were spiritual, intellectual, and emotional, leading to the discovery of inner integrity and self-acceptance.

Gino's life was a testament to the power of essence over ego. He was remarkably disciplined, having studied Latin for four years in high school, during which he limited his recreation time to just 30 minutes a week, making more time for learning and self-development. He wasn't concerned with social conventions but followed his own path with unwavering clarity. Gino listened to opera, appreciated the beauty in the world, and understood both poverty and privilege, all while maintaining a humble and academic demeanor that he would carry through his long, distinguished career as the Founder of the Department of Religion and Professor Emeritus in the Henry M. Jackson School of International Studies at the University of Washington. He didn't need anyone's approval, making his presence unique and inspiring. He didn't let his ego prevent him from showing the world what he stood for.

I deeply admired my brother's sovereignty—a term I use to describe his independence and self-governance. He wasn't swayed by others' opinions, living with a sense of purpose transcending ego. He showed me that ego could be frivolous and distracting while essence invited a deeper conversation with life itself. Gino valued me not for my looks or any superficial qualities but for the soulful essence he saw within me, the same essence he cherished in himself.

My relationship with Gino allowed me to discover how essence, rather than ego, defines a person. It's not about self-importance or external achievements but about the authenticity and purity we bring to our interactions. This realization helped me navigate my own journey from ego to essence, understanding that my worth wasn't defined by societal standards or others' opinions but by the light only I could bring into the world.

UNDERSTANDING ESSENCE AND THE CORE OF OUR BEING

Through my brother Gino, I understood that essence is the core of what we come into this world with—our values, purpose, and the unique traits that make us who we are. There is a vast connection that goes beyond the measurable or material, touching on the purity of our spirit and the very essence of our character. This essence is the promise of all we are meant to share with the world, the unique contribution only we can make. When we think about the things people love us for, it is always our essence, gifts, talents, and uniqueness. The world needs more of these qualities. If you take a moment, you will likely agree that when you are in the state of expressing your talents, giving your gifts, exuding your essence, and basking in your uniqueness, you feel elevated and enriched.

In the words of Buckminster Fuller, one of the greatest visionaries of our time: "You do not belong to you. You belong to the Universe... Never forget that you are one of a kind." This quote encapsulates the idea that our essence is not ours to hide but to share with the world, to use in service of the greater good. We are here to light up the world with our unique gifts, much like my brother inspired through his quiet strength and wisdom, my grandmother who delighted others with her cooking, and my daughter who shows in her care and devotion to her clients, our essence is what brings about greater love and deeper connections.

Our essence is our Divine spark, a reflection of our true nature, unencumbered by the superficial demands of the ego. It is the part of us that remains honest and true, no matter the external circumstances. When we tap into our essence, we tap into a limitless source of creativity, compassion, and empowerment. We understand that our purpose is not just about what we achieve but *how* we live and *who* we become in the process.

To live from essence versus ego is to honor the Divine promise of gifts born within you and let them blossom in all you do. It is also about recognizing that each moment is an opportunity to share your authentic self with the world and to make a difference simply by being who you are. When you do this, you enrich your own life and inspire others to do the same, enabling them to live in their essence. This mirroring of our true selves perpetuates the magic of living from essence and guarantees a life of fulfillment, joy, and greater impact.

PRACTICAL STEPS TO EMBRACE YOUR ESSENCE

Allow me to share several tools and exercises I have learned over the years on connecting with one's truest essence. Some of these suggestions I learned from Gino, Alice, my friends, and important loved ones. All of them are practices I have used to dip into the essence of who I am and, in turn, cultivate in others. I invite you to try each one to see which resonates with you. You'll never know if it works unless you give it your honest effort. What we are told to enjoy versus what we intrinsically love can often differ. Listen to your essence and forget what the ego demands. Go outside the familiar and venture into the depth of what makes you, you.

Intuitive Journaling

- I love journaling! It is a practice that allows us to explore our thoughts and feelings safely. By asking questions and listening for answers, we can engage in a dialogue with our Higher Self or a wisdom figure, connecting with the essence we know to be true.

Being Outdoors

- I recommend surrounding yourself with beauty through nature, art, or meaningful conversations. These moments of natural grace remind us of the *magic* attracted to essence, not ego. When we are true to ourselves, immersed in beauty, nature, and human connection, we invite *magic* into our lives in more heart-centered and profound ways.

Self Reflection

· Another powerful exercise is to reflect on a time when you felt most fully alive, most yourself. *What were you doing? Who were you with? What qualities were you embodying?* These moments are clues to your essence, guiding you back to your authentic self whenever you feel lost or disconnected.

The journey from ego to essence is about shedding the layers of protection we've built around ourselves. It's a continuous process of self-discovery, where we learn to distinguish between the ego's voice and the quiet wisdom within. By embracing this distinction, we align ourselves with our true selves and shine in our greatest light.

Living in alignment with your essence means being true to who you are, even when it's challenging. It's about finding the courage to express your unique gifts and to honor the Divine gifts within you. Living from this place of authenticity makes you an irresistible magnet for the right people, opportunities, and experiences. The Universe responds to your truth, and *magic* unfolds in ways you never could have expected.

As you explore and embrace your essence, remember that this path is only sometimes well-paved or clearly marked. There will be moments when the pull of the ego feels stronger, when fear and doubt may cloud your vision, and when you revert to old habits of letting your ego rule over your essence. In these times, be gentle with yourself. Understand that moving from ego to essence is an ongoing practice that requires patience, compassion, and a willingness to expand beyond what has been comfortable.

I encourage you to take a moment each day to reconnect with your heart, honor your unique place in this world, and let your essence be your compass. The world wants to experience the magic that only you can bring. When you live from your essence, you fulfill your inborn promise in a profound and irreplaceable way. Each small step toward your true self is a victory, no matter how subtle it may seem. By choosing authenticity over approval, connection over comparison, and love over fear, you align more closely with who you are meant to be. With each choice you make, you build a life that isn't about traditional success but about fulfillment, joy, and a deep, unwavering self-acceptance.

Your essence is your greatest gift to the world. By nurturing it, you enrich your own life and spark others to do the same. The more you show up as your essence, the more you create a ripple effect for others to do the same. This is how each of us can collectively raise the world's consciousness. By stepping beyond our ego and into our truth, living from our authentic hearts, we spark more *magic* into existence.

"The privilege of a lifetime is to become who you truly are."

—CARL JUNG

Chapter 3

Dance with Destiny

I'm convinced one's destiny is not a rigid path set in stone but a fluid journey woven within the threads of every choice and breath we take. Like a dance, destiny moves gracefully through the rhythms of life, filled with unexpected turns, wild surprises, and tender moments, equalling *magic* in motion. To truly *dance with destiny* is to expect and welcome this unpredictable magic—to open ourselves to the flow of possibility, to trust in unseen forces guiding us, and to step forward with faith, even when we don't know where the 'direction' will take us.

I know that many people struggle with the idea of destiny, believing instead that life is a series of random events that we must *control* to achieve our goals. For them, the concept of *magic* guiding their journey seems unrealistic or too abstract. They prefer certainty, fear the unexplainable, and rely on rigid plans and guarantees to feel secure. In living this way, they close themselves off to the unexpected wonders life offers. They miss the serendipitous moments, the synchronicities, and the gentle nudges from the Universe that are here to guide us if we are willing to believe and allow.

It has become apparent to me that when we resist the flow of destiny, we deny ourselves the full experience of what life can be. We become so focused on what we 'think we want' or what we 'believe is best' that we fail to see the *magic* that happens naturally when we remain open and expectant. Such resistance stems from a place of fear—a fear of surrendering to the unknown and the undefined. Yet, it is in moments of surrender when we allow the *magic* to show us the way that our true path, or destiny, reveals itself.

If I have learned one masterful tip I have used consistently throughout my life, it is that by *letting go* of our need to control every outcome, we invite a deeper connection with our destiny and open ourselves to the infinite opportunities that await. And, when we embrace life's journey with an open heart, we align ourselves with a greater outcome, allowing the *magic* of our destiny to transpire in ways far beyond our expectations. I have found that when we are prompted to trust in a feeling or a knowing, it often brings synchronous events. It is as if the Universe is speaking directly to us, guiding us toward our destiny if we are willing to listen and surrender. This dance is not always easy.

It requires letting go of our outward governance, submitting to the cosmic flow, and sensing that even in moments of uncertainty, there is an opportunity just waiting to awaken us.

Dancing with destiny calls for courage, trust, and a willingness to embrace the unknown. The more we release our need to control every outcome, the more we invite unexpected wonders to unfold.

Your destiny is not something to force or chase. It is an evolving journey that reveals itself in the quiet moments of surrender and faith. With each step you take, trust that *magic* guides you toward possibilities greater than anything you could have planned. Dancing with destiny is about moving with ease and allowing rather than forcing or maneuvering. A natural ease comes from working with the flow instead of against it. The most fluid and harmonious outcomes emerge when you trust the rhythm and let yourself be guided. Your role is not to control every turn but to stay open, responsive, and present. With each step, you create a beautiful partnership with the *unfolding* of your destiny,

TRUSTING THE FLOW OF LIFE

In my early twenties, I learned the lesson of dancing with destiny in a way that would forever shape my life. At 21, I was engaged to be married after dating my fiancé for over a year. But despite the security and comfort that relationship offered, I had a sudden and undeniable knowing that it wasn't right for me. It wasn't that anything was wrong with him or us; it was simply that deep in my heart, I knew he would not be able to love me how I yearned to be cared for. He lacked a capacity for true intimacy, of sharing his whole heart with me. I wanted a deep feeling of oneness, a connection that resonated with the belief in my heart that true, unequivocal love was part of my destiny. In a moment of clarity and conviction, I called off the engagement, trusting that this was the right decision. I let go of what seemed secure and stepped into the unknown, willing to embrace my *true* destiny.

Within days after that breakup, I unexpectedly traveled to Hong Kong with my parents. I had not planned to go with them, but the ending of my engagement left me free to go on a trip and an opportunity to reinvigorate myself. That journey would change my life forever and solidify the knowing that when we dance with situations, move from one place to the next, and soften to the unanticipated rhythms life presents, *magic* is most definitely at work.

On my first day in Hong Kong, before the hotel restaurant opened, I felt an inexplicable urge to get dressed up and venture to the lobby to enjoy its opulence. I didn't know why, but I trusted that feeling and inner prompting and listened to the nudge. As I stood inside the hotel entrance, unsure but expectant, a handsome businessman carrying a briefcase walked out of the elevator. The business associate with him was suddenly called away, leaving him alone in the lobby with me. Without any provocation, he walked over, and at that moment, I felt a magnetic pull and knew my destiny was about to materialize.

I remember being shy, almost afraid to look at him, but something deeper within me knew our encounter was meant to be. He politely asked where I was from and asked a few other endearing questions, including an invitation to coffee in the restaurant rooftop that afternoon. That magical moment was the beginning of it all; three days later, we were engaged, and Paul von Welanetz became the love of my life and husband for the next twenty-five years. Our meeting in that lobby on that day in Hong Kong was 100% *magic*, debuting our destiny! *Tah-Dah!* It was a dance with destiny that I could not have orchestrated myself. It was as if the Universe had erupted to bring us together, and I knew that by trusting my intuition and following the signs, I had aligned myself with my future.

That experience taught me that there is a place within each of us that knows everything—a deep well of wisdom and intuition that guides us if we are willing to listen. Such inner knowing isn't bound by logic or external validation; it's a profound sense of understanding that resides deep within our hearts. Dawna Markova, a brilliant thinker and author who explores human potential and the mysteries of consciousness, often talks about the incredible promise we all have within us. She references Erik Erikson, the renowned developmental psychologist who once uniquely demonstrated this inner power to a class he taught. During a lecture at Columbia University, Erikson was challenged by the faculty to secretly hypnotize a student in a large audience simply by placing a dot under their chair—no words, just a symbol of dynamic focus. Not knowing the dot was under her seat, the student was hypnotized throughout the class. That student was Dawna Markova, and that moment set the trajectory for her future studies and devoted life's work.

Such a profound interaction demonstrates the vast, untapped reservoir of insight and intuition that lies beyond our conscious minds. It's a reminder that there's a space within us that holds profound knowledge and that our inner guidance is always there, waiting for us to trust it and let it lead the way. We all have this inner guidance, a place within us where every answer resides. This space is not clouded by doubt or fear but instead is a pure connection to our true selves, a direct line to the Universe's infinite reservoir. When we tap into this place, we open ourselves to information that is not just intellectual but an innate knowing that encompasses our entire being. It's where our intuition speaks loudest and where our true desires become clear, even when the outside world offers contrast or contradiction.

Admittedly, accessing this inner wisdom requires stillness and trust. Many of us are so caught up in the noise of daily life, the endless stream of thoughts and worries, that we forget to pause and listen to what's inside. We doubt our internal feelings, question our intuition, and rely on external opinions and societal expectations. If we can quiet the mind and turn inward, we can find the answers we need. Our inner connection is our access point to the *magic* we have within and the ability to co-create with our destiny.

As you read these words, *The Sacred Dance of Life* by Hafiz, envision the *magic* of life unfolding. Invite and encourage your inner voice to speak freely, allowing it to lead you toward your destiny. By cultivating a practice of tuning into your inner knowing, you can navigate life with a sense of ease and confidence. You can learn to trust the subtle nudges and feelings that guide you, recognizing them as the *language of the soul,* pulled by destiny. This doesn't mean that life becomes predictable or free of challenges, but rather that you move through it with a sense of partnership with *All That Is*, a dance if you like, trusting that your inner self is guiding every step you take.

The Sacred Dance for Life
—Hafiz

I sometimes forget
that I was created for Joy.

My mind is too busy.

My Heart is too heavy
for me to remember
that I have been

called to dance
the Sacred dance of life.

I was created to smile
To Love
To be lifted up
And to lift others up.

O' Sacred One
Untangle my feet
from all that ensnares.

Free my soul.

That we might
Dance
and that our dancing
might be contagious.

THE ART OF TRUSTING

Dancing with destiny is not just *waiting* for what we want; it's about aligning with the energy of creation itself. *Magic* is not a stiff, unyielding force. It's fluid, like a dance, arriving through creative flow and aligned movement. It is the art of knowing, believing, letting go, and trusting. When we dance, we surrender to something beyond our-selves, like a note on the wind, a tune vibrating in the eardrum, or a melody that seeps beneath the skin. It is an act of faith, an embrace of the unknown, and a deep understanding that *everything* unfolds in perfect timing and alignment.

Of course, when I say everything, I mean *everything*, not just the bliss of a romance or the high of a big success, but the challenges and obstacles of life that often appear. In my dance with destiny, I've learned that difficulty and hardship often preclude opportunity and potential. Every setback, every moment of pain or uncertainty, is an invitation to grow, learn, and expand. I have always been good at maneuvering through challenges, seeing them not as obstacles but stepping stones toward something greater. As the saying goes, "No breakdown, no breakthrough." The greatest opportunities arise through the sudden changes and challenges, fostering a deeper rev-erence for what is about to unfold.

Amidst a wonderful marriage and magical love life, Paul and I faced many hurdles and setbacks. Life wasn't perfect or all mapped out. We had to endure tough times and unforeseen circumstances. We needed to hang on tight, weave, and maneuver to emerge victorious. Luckily, I married a man who was a great dancer, not just on the dance floor but in life itself. He was trained by dance legend Arthur Murray, and through that training, Paul taught me the most exquisite ways of living, loving, and dancing *with* life. Paul was an artist, deeply sensitive, always reading, and constantly expanding his knowledge. Fourteen years my senior, he introduced me to a life of flow, rhythm, grace, and elegance. He helped create the electricity of magic that filled our lives and became a part of our relationship for over two decades because he trusted life itself.

Together, we let go of needing to know and control every outcome. We opened ourselves to possibilities and embraced change. We pivoted when we had to and hunkered close through each storm with a deep belief that everything was happening exactly as it should. During those twenty-five years, we overcame challenges and trusted our destiny. We published six award-winning cookbooks together and were recognized for their unique blend of joyful celebration and delicious menus. I was featured in *House and Garden* magazine alongside Martha Stewart as the most prominent lifestyle 'experts East and West,' but even that entrepreneurial journey was not without its difficulties. We faced setbacks, including the threat of losing our cooking show, which forced us to reinvent ourselves, lean into our spirituality, and know that something *more* was beckoning.

Paul and I began looking for ways to serve others, particularly those who wanted a better future for the world. That led us to attend a mastermind group called *Impact* in Hollywood. Participants were encouraged to set bold, seemingly unreachable goals and believe with great conviction that they would materialize. Paul and I set our goal, and within three days, we achieved what we once thought was impossible. That experience taught us the *magic of intention*, the power of believing wholeheartedly, and that, in the end, only the action you actually take matters. It also showed us that forces are working *with* us and *for* us to shape our destiny.

That undeniable experience of reaching an outrageous goal in such a short time led to Paul and I founding the *Inside Edge Foundation for Education*. It started as a breakfast networking organization that hosted speakers in person. We began by gathering people around tables to connect and applaud each other, but we no longer needed to cook the food. More than 1,700 of the world's greatest thought leaders and visionaries came together to convey their knowledge and add to the collective consciousness. The *Inside Edge* expanded from the Beverly Hills Hotel to three Southern California cities. It became the number one place for forward-thinking leaders to emerge, all because we learned how to align ourselves with our truest and highest purpose and to dance with our destiny.

The *Inside Edge* was an idea born from our willingness to open ourselves to what was next, what was ready to come forth, and what was calling us. It has continued for over thirty-nine years, inspiring the next generation of thought leaders and changemakers. Its enduring success is a testament to the power of letting go, releasing who we thought we should be and what we thought we should do, and aligning with our highest purpose. When we stopped forcing outcomes and trusted the flow of what wanted to emerge, *magic* happened. The

Inside Edge became more than an organization. It grew into a living testament to what is possible when we commit to the unfolding of our journey, allowing destiny to shape something more extraordinary than we could have imagined.

Our experience shows that not always 'knowing' allows *magic* to transpire. That means I encourage you to perceive both the unknown and the difficulties as opportunities for growth and discovery. The Chinese ideogram for *crisis* is composed of two characters: one representing *danger* and the other representing *opportunity*. In many ways, danger can be reframed to become opportunity if we open our minds to the idea that the 'yet-to-be-experienced' is a wide-open invitation for *magic* to appear. Within every crisis lies the potential unfoldment of yet-to-be-discovered possibilities. To dance with destiny is to live with the sensitivity to trust the calling of your life's journey and believe that magic is guiding you directly toward your most joy-filled destiny.

WAYS TO DANCE WITH DESTINY

You have a hand in your destiny. You can turn on the music, raise the volume, and step boldly onto the dance floor. Even if you don't know every song, you can choose to move to the beat with confidence and trust. By adapting, maneuvering, and staying connected, you create a stronger bond with the destiny meant for you. You can deepen your connection and influence how your journey unfolds through intentional actions and thoughtful choices.

One powerful way to deepen your connection with your destiny is to begin a *Divine Dialogue* between yourself and any project, relationship, or wisdom figures you are drawn to. *Divine Dialogue* is a unique technique I developed after years of learning how accessible life's answers are to each of us. With *intention comes direction; depending* on where we seek guidance, there are answers just waiting to be heard.

Divine Dialogue involves letting go of the rigid need for specific answers and allowing messages and deep knowing to emerge from a place beyond ego, fact, or the logical mind. It requires trust, curiosity, and a willingness to explore the wisdom within and around you. Throughout my life, I have engaged in this practice, connecting with the energy of loved ones, both living and no longer with us, mentors, and even the spirit of a project or decision I was facing. Regardless of the physical proximity or form, I've found that when I ask with genuine intention, the guidance I need always finds its way to me.

Wisdom, answers, and direction will come to us when we are receptive and listening. We simply need to center into stillness, set the intention, and be willing to hear what is available to assist us. This dialogue is not about forcing an answer or seeking immediate clarity. It is about allowing our destiny to flow in its own time. It's a partnership between you and the unseen forces at work in your life. When you trust this process, you access a deep reservoir of guidance, insights, and inspiration to help you move forward with clarity and confidence.

Divine Dialogue is a means of letting go of the need for control and opening your heart to the messages waiting to be shared. It invites you to create space for reflection and discovery, whether that comes through journaling, meditation, prayer, or simply sitting quietly with your intention. This practice reminds us that we are never alone on our journey. We are always supported, always connected, and always guided toward the next step in our destiny when we choose to connect.

Here's how to practice *Divine Dialogue* with a project or relationship from which you wish to receive answers:

1. **Dialogue with Your Work or Relationship:** Start by writing ten stepping stones or pivotal points that represent the life of a project or the relationship. Conceptualize the journey, major points, or key steps it took you to get to where you are *now*. Use compassion and heartfelt context to establish these points and write them down.

2. **Reflect on Your Path:** Open your understanding to everything that has led you to the present moment in your work or that relationship.

Allow this exercise to help you see the bigger picture and understand the Divine timing of your journey. Factor in trust and density to each stepping point and soften any edges or annexes surrounding these steps. Often, hindsight and reflection can widen our views and give us a clearer understanding of past events. Seeing things from a higher vantage point will give you a clearer perspective of the reason those steps were taken.

3. **Create a Focusing Statement:** Once you have clarity on the journey, create a statement about *why* this project or relationship matters. *Why are you beginning this dialogue at this precise moment? What is its highest purpose? What is the unique contribution your work together will make to your life and the world?* Ask expansive, open-ended questions that empower profound access.

4. **Ask the Work or Relationship What It Wants:** This may sound unusual, but ask your project or relationship what *it* wants. Listen for Divine Guidance and write down what comes through. Be attentive to the messages, trusting they lead you toward your highest good.

5. **Trust the Process:** The word 'expect' sets the tone for trusting the process. Your receptivity and comfort will influence the clairvoyant information that comes through. Know that when you let go of control and open yourself to the flow of your destiny, *magic* will unfold and give you the exact answers you were yearning to hear.

As you navigate this path of *Divine Dialogue, you are building a connection to your soul and your deeper essence.* Remember that listening is key. Quieting the mind, discarding doubt, and eliminating skepticism will make room for Divine answers to appear. A universal dance is happening, so allow it to welcome you into its arms without judgment or impatience. To fully dance with destiny is to live with an open heart, embrace each moment as it comes, and sense the knowing that everything is unfolding perfectly as it should.

"Make no judgments.
Make no comparisons.
Delete your need for understanding."

—BRUGH JOY

Chapter 4

Nurture Ourselves with Thoughts

I hope you have enjoyed what you've read so far and that much of what I'm sharing resonates with you. Perhaps some of it is connecting with your deeper knowing, while other parts may be challenging your preconceived beliefs. You might find yourself wholeheartedly with me, or perhaps you're holding back, still undecided about what to think. This freedom to explore, to agree or disagree, is the beauty of the mind. It is the power to choose, the ability to question, and the freedom to evaluate new concepts.

Countless scholars have said that one of the great truths of life is the power we have to *choose our thoughts*. This is not an abstract concept rooted in spirituality; Viktor Frankl, in his seminal book *Man's Search for Meaning*, so poignantly illuminated this truth. Enduring the unimaginable horrors of a concentration camp, he came to understand that while we cannot always control our circumstances, we can always *choose* our mental fortitude. Frankl's discipline and conviction teach us that light is always possible if we *choose* to see it, no matter how dark things appear. The choice in how we think or perceive our world is the first step toward nurturing our thoughts and ourselves.

In his 1903 book *As a Man Thinketh*, James Allen wrote, "The mind is like a garden which can be intelligently cultivated or allowed to run wild." Similarly, an anonymous proverb states, "Your mind is a garden. Your thoughts are the seeds. You can grow flowers, or you can grow weeds."

The power of nurturing our thoughts lies in how we *choose* to cultivate them. *Are we planting seeds of hope, love, and possibility, or are we allowing weeds of fear and worry to take root?* Nurturing ourselves with thoughts means consciously tending to the soil of our minds, weeding out what no longer serves us, and watering ideas that elevate our lives.

One of the most powerful practices we can cultivate is the ability to choose our thoughts *consciously*. So often, we let our thoughts run rampant, allowing them to dictate our mood, our energy, and even our sense of self-worth. *But what if we* deliberately chose *what we wanted to think? What if we chose thoughts of possibility, hope, and love instead of allowing worry and fear to dominate?* Like the emotion of *joy* shared in chapter one, feelings of the highest vibration serve as a compass, guiding us toward a life of alignment and flow. When we tune our thoughts to these higher frequencies, we resonate with Divine energy, attracting more of what feels expansive and playful.

Many feel their thoughts are out of their control. Like random patterns, they feel forced to live with conditioning, programmed by the past, or dictated by the world around them. They believe their thinking is something beyond their governance, a way of being they must simply endure. In adhering to this belief, many relinquish their innate power to consciously choose what they want to believe and how they prefer to think. They fail to realize that our thoughts are not fixed, and we are not victims of our minds. We have the right and the ability to direct our thinking toward thoughts that serve us, uplift us, and align with the lifestyle we truly desire.

CHOOSING OUR THOUGHTS, NURTURING OUR SPIRIT

Choosing our thoughts isn't just about thinking positively; it's about creating a nurturing environment where our mindset can flourish. The more we consciously choose thoughts that elevate us, the more we feed our soul with the nourishment it craves—*peace*, *purpose*, and Divine *possibility*. Every time we choose a thought that uplifts us, we step further into our actualization and divine essence.

You are never at the mercy of your thoughts. You have the right to choose *what* you believe and *how* you think. This power to shape your inner world has always been within you, and as you embrace it, you will see just how often and acutely *magic* unfolds in your life. The thoughts you nurture are the seeds of the reality you create. Research and experience alike have shown that positive thoughts lead to positive outcomes, revealing the transformative power of your mindset.

Unfortunately, on the opposite side of positive thoughts are emotions at the lowest end of the spectrum: *fear*, *anger*, *shame*, and *doubt*. These emotions are deeply intertwined with the ego and our human conditioning. While often well-intentioned in its desire to protect us, the ego keeps us rooted in survival mode, where everything feels like a threat or burden. The ego feeds on fear, thrives in judgment, and clings to control, creating a continual sense of insufficiency.

When we sink into these lower vibrations, we allow our ego-driven thoughts to take the lead. Such emotions cloud our judgment, disconnect us from our intuition, and keep us trapped in a cycle of worry and negativity. The ego tells us we must *strive*, *fight*, and *defend*. It convinces us that we are separate from others and that life is a series of battles to be won or lost. But in truth, this is the most limiting perspective of all. The ego's focus on fear and control blocks the flow of joy, creativity, and abundance, the very things we yearn for.

The ego is not our enemy but a small and often misguided part of ourselves that operates from a place of distrust. Its view is narrow, unable to see the full picture, and it fixates on what could go wrong rather than right. We forget our true power when we are in the ego's grip. We abandon the knowing that we are co-creators of our reality. Instead of seeing opportunities, we see obstacles. Instead of hope, we feel hopelessness.

When we live in these lower vibrations, we operate in a state of contraction, where everything feels heavy, overwhelming, and out of reach – the opposite of *magic*. The ego needs stability, control, and predictability, whereas *magic* needs freedom, faith, and won-derment. When faced with uncertainty, the ego jumps at the chance to spiral into anxiety or even despair because it cannot tolerate the unknown. The ego convinces us that every deviation from the plan is dangerous and every challenge is insurmountable. But the ego doesn't have the full picture. It's like a well-meaning but misguided friend, trying to help but often leading us down the wrong path. Our work is to *choose our thoughts* and gently remind ourselves there is a higher wisdom available. When we cultivate our thoughts and are conscious of our power to do so, we move away from lack and find the plentiful.

The moment we become aware of our ego taking over, we can shift our thoughts to taming it. We can soften its grip by turning our thoughts inward, breathing deeply, and remembering that we are *not* our fears. We are expansive beings capable of choosing love over fear, hope over despair, and peace over anxiety. All of that is a choice. The key is to be alert, notice where our thoughts are taking over, and then consciously course-correct. If we are spiraling into worry and control, we can *choose* to perceive things differently from a place of trust and openness.

Shifting our thoughts takes the thought of being willing to shift. Think about it; we must first think about bringing it into being. Then, as we embrace the new thought, shifts occur, and we free ourselves from ego's limitations and return to higher vibrations of our true essence. This new thought creation is the journey from ego to spirit, and it begins with the simple but powerful *choice* of where we direct our thoughts.

THE POWER OF WONDER

When we move beyond the confines of our ego, we enter the realm of wonder and awe. This is where *magic* truly happens. This is when we can see life with fresh eyes and embrace everything as being more than what it seems. We stop resisting reality or 'wishing' for things to be different, and instead, we open ourselves to the gifts of the present moment, no matter how challenging they may be. Here, in this space of openness, we begin to ask powerful questions like, *"What if this challenge is actually a gift?"* or *"What if it's leading me to something greater than I can yet imagine?"* This is the doorway to transformation. These *what if* questions allow us to choose our thoughts and see how life conspires in our favor, even in the hardest moments.

What if questions are like keys that unlock our thoughts and awaken the realm of possibility. They take us beyond the narrow, fear-driven perspective of the ego and open us up to expansive potential. *What if* questions invite us to dream again, to believe in the unseen, and to *choose to trust* that there is more to our lives than what we can perceive in any given moment? When we ask, *"What if I could see this situation more spaciously?"* or *"What if I can choose thoughts that create a whole new reality?"* we are not just imagining a better outcome but choosing enlivening possibilities for our lives. We are signaling our desire for something greater and our willingness to let go of limitations and step into a place of trust and expansion.

What if questions have become an essential part of my daily life. They are the cornerstone of moving beyond ego-driven moments and *choosing* to transport myself into new realms waiting to be discovered. Whenever I face a difficult situation or feel overwhelmed by challenges that seem insurmountable, I turn to *What if* questions to shift my perspective by simply asking, *"What if I break through the confines my ego has built, allowing something new to capture my attention and guide me in a fresh, more expansive direction?"* I find a powerful way to step into the *magic* of what else can be.

I invite you to shift your thinking, choose your thoughts, and embrace *what if* questions whenever you feel stuck, backed into a corner, or uncertain about your next step. In those moments of typical thoughts, take a deep breath and ask yourself *what if,* followed by an open-ended question. This simple practice awakens the magical forces that are always waiting to support you. *what if* questions signal our minds to move outside of habitual thinking or ego-driven perspective, allowing us to contemplate and ultimately choose a different thought. These purposeful questions provide insight into new solutions and bypass the ego that is stuck in thinking the way it has always thought.

To practice the power of *what if* questions, try this simple exercise:

1. **Identify the Challenge or Fear:**
   - Start by bringing to mind a challenge or fear that has been weighing on you. It can be anything disturbing, such as a difficult relationship, a work situation, or an uncomfortable personal fear.

2. **Acknowledge Your Current Perspective:**
   - Notice how your ego views the situation. *Are you stuck in worry, doubt, or fear? Are you convinced that things won't improve or that the challenge is too great? Do you feel this*

very moment would be great for taking a nap? Acknowledge the thoughts and feelings that are currently dominating your mind without judgment. Take a deep breath and set an intention to welcome something new.

3. **Shift into Curiosity with *what if* Questions:**

   - Ask yourself *what if* questions that open up the possibility for something new. For example:
     - *What if* this challenge is exactly what I need to grow?
     - *What if* this situation is teaching me something invaluable?
     - *What if* this obstacle is clearing the way for something better?
     - *What if* events are unfolding in perfect timing, even if I don't see that yet?

These questions don't require immediate answers. The power lies in the asking. Each question invites a shift in perspective that releases the ego's grip and ventures into a state of openness and possibility.

4. **Notice the Emotional Shift:**

   - As you ask these *what if* questions, pay attention to how your body and emotions respond. *Do you feel a lightness, a sense of relief, or maybe even excitement?* This is the *magic* of *what if*: It lifts you out of fear and into a higher vibration where solutions, ideas, and clarity flow.

5. Journal Your Reflections:

- After completing this exercise, take a few moments to journal about the experience. *How did your initial thoughts about the situation change? Did you feel more hopeful, empowered, or at peace? What new insights came to you as you asked these questions?*

This exercise is a simple yet powerful way to nurture ourselves with thoughts that serve us. By shifting from *"Why is this happening to me?"* to *"What if this is happening for me?"* we reclaim our power.

The beauty of *what if* questions is that the ego's limited vision does not bind them. They allow us to dream without restriction, imagine without fear, and be open to a future filled with magical potential. These questions awaken curiosity, and we are no longer afraid when we are curious. We are no longer resisting life. We are participating in, co-creating, and counting on more to be revealed.

ASKING THE MAGICAL *WHAT IF?*

If the thoughts we choose are seeds we plant in the garden of our minds, then, like any good gardener, we must be intentional about what we cultivate. Every thought can shape our experience, so choose carefully. When you nurture yourself with thoughts of hope, love, and possibility, the *magic* of life unfolds effortlessly before you. It is as if the Universe has been waiting for you to ask all along.

What if is such a simple question yet holds incredible power. It encourages us to open ourselves to possibilities we might not have considered before. It is how we lift the veil of limitation and invite a childlike sense of curiosity and wonder into our lives.

The beauty of asking *what if* lies in its expansiveness. It doesn't require an immediate answer or force a solution. Instead, it taps into a higher consciousness, inviting the light of new possibilities to pour in. It softens the edges of our fears, loosens the ego's grip, and invites grace to step in. Often, in perfect Divine timing, answers and solutions reveal themselves gently when we least expect them, like flowers blooming, allowing us to choose which one we will pick.

I encourage you to pause today and ask: *What if today is the day things shift? What if I can find peace right where I am? What if the best is yet to come, and this is just the beginning?* These simple yet profound questions are not only invitations for *magic;* they are the first steps in transforming your reality. It all starts with a thought, and the thoughts you choose today shape the beauty and promise of tomorrow. *What if this challenge is actually here to guide me? What if something beautiful is waiting for me on the other side of this struggle? What if the Universe knows this circumstance is best for me?* These questions aren't just idle wonderings; they are keys that unlock the door to new realities.

THE JOURNEY FROM EGO TO ESSENCE

Ultimately, the key to nurturing ourselves with thoughts is to ask the 'right' questions. *What If* questions are a bridge that takes us from fear to faith, from doubt to wonder. They remind us that we are powerful creators capable of shifting our reality with the thoughts we choose.

Reflecting on my own journey, I remember when I thought I knew exactly what my life should look like. I had envisioned myself as a mother of five, fully immersed in motherhood. Yet, life had other plans. After Paul and I had our first child, Lexi, I was thrown into a state of overwhelm, deep in postpartum depression, without even knowing that's what it was. During the first months following her birth, I faced a darkness I wasn't prepared for and lost a large part of myself in the expectations and demands that motherhood placed on me.

It was then I gradually discovered there is beauty in darkness, learning, expanding, and being forced into a metamorphosis—becoming someone entirely new. In despair and self-loathing, I entered a cocoon that changed me on a cellular level. In that despair, something beautiful began to take shape, and it all began with one powerful *what if* question I asked myself. *"What if I explore how to improve this situation?"*

Being home with Lexi had me asking, *What if, instead of just feeding the baby and feeling housebound, I expand my love for cooking and inviting people into my kitchen—sharing meals and stories and creating a sense of community around food?* At first, it felt like a way to distract myself, to fill the void left by the isolation I was experiencing as a new mother. But over time, I realized how these *what if* questions offer so much more. Cooking had been my lifelong passion, and it then became a healing ritual and a way to nurture myself and those around me. I found *magic* in an unexpected place, all because of a simple question: *What if the life I thought I wanted was now leading me into even broader fulfillment?*

That question opened up a new vision for my life. Several friends, when stopping by to see the baby, noticed the treats I'd prepared and asked me to teach them techniques and recipes I'd learned when I attended culinary classes in Paris and years of classes with a chef in Beverly Hills. Magically, I no longer needed multiple children to feel complete or to meet others' expectations. I began to see my future differently, leaning into my strengths instead of clinging to unrealistic ideals. I stepped into the possibility that maybe life was meant to unfold in a unique new way and past conditioning did not bind me.

Those *what if* questions led to many more, and I rapidly embraced a shift within myself. I began focusing on what was good in my life rather than being consumed by my 'shoulds.' I let go of the pressure to be the 'perfect' or 'traditional' mother and expanded my view of what would truly make me and those around me happy. By doing so, I became a more present mother to Lexi and a better partner to Paul.

I'd found a new way of being that allowed me to thrive in innate talents and freed me from outdated roles and expectations.

Of course, that was just the beginning of what became a very successful and deeply rewarding career in cooking. Paul and I went on to produce a critically acclaimed television cooking show, write six cookbooks, and receive numerous awards and features in major publications. We thrived in the culinary world, and the experience brought us even closer as we worked side by side for many years. It wasn't just about our professional success but about how that path allowed us to grow as a family. Lexi enjoyed her parents in ways that traditional motherhood or a typical economic path might not have afforded us. Becoming an expert in cooking and entertaining became the bond that enriched our lives, giving us the freedom to create together and live more fully. And it all began with one poignant *what if*?

This is the power of asking *what if*? It's a magical process because it invites unbounded possibility. We open ourselves up to anything and everything that can possibly transpire. Thus, the mundane becomes magical by asking, *what if* we start to see the world not as something to be controlled by us, but as something to be dazzled by?

The next time you feel stuck in fear, overwhelmed by circumstances, or disconnected from hope, pause and ask yourself: *"What if there is more to this than I can see right now? What if I am being guided toward something greater? What if I am on the verge of a miracle?"*

These questions are not just fantasies but invitations for magic to enter your life. You find yourself gifted with a vast cornucopia of all life has to offer.

THOUGHTS = EMOTIONS = ACTIONS

The promise of *what if* questions is that they can instantly change our thoughts. Since our thoughts are instantly connected to our emotions, those emotions, in turn, prompt our actions and reactions. It's a seamless, often unconscious process; one question sparks a feeling, and that feeling compels us to respond, whether we realize it or not. This cycle happens so quickly that we may not even realize how profoundly our inner world shapes our external reality.

When we think of something positive or negative, our brain releases chemicals that match that thought. Suppose we think of something joyful, like soft, affectionate baby kittens. Our brain releases feel-good hormones like serotonin and dopamine, which create feelings of calm, happiness, and peace. Our body relaxes, and we're more likely to respond to the world around us with openness, kindness, and patience. We smile more, engage more easily with others, and feel more connected to the benefits of life.

Now, contrast that with a darker thought, like the image of a stormy sky over a funeral plot. Sensing danger or distress, the brain releases stress hormones like cortisol and adrenaline. These chemicals trigger feelings of anxiety, fear, or sadness. Our body tenses, our heart rate increases, and suddenly, our reactions become more defensive and closed off. We may snap at someone, withdraw, or feel overwhelmed by even the smallest challenges. The entire atmosphere of our day shifts because of that one seemingly small thought.

This connection between thought, emotion, and action is so powerful that it can shape the course of our lives. Imagine your thoughts being consistently rooted in negativity or anxiety. Day after day, such thoughts create feelings of conflict and insecurity. Over time, this becomes your default emotional state, and how you engage with others and approach challenges is colored by that emotional lens. You find yourself making decisions from a place of limitation, avoiding risks, and distrusting opportunities. Your thoughts create a reality where limitations dictate your choices.

Alternatively, if you choose to focus on thoughts of hope, love, or empowerment, your emotional state becomes one of confidence, openness, and ingenuity. You'll find yourself taking inspired action, moving toward your goals with trust instead of fear, and navigating life's challenges with resilience. Your reactions to the world are then shaped by an inner sense of calm and optimism; as a result, the world reflects positive energy back at you.

This beautiful reciprocal cycle is born through the simple but profound practice of *choosing* our thoughts. By becoming mindful of what we think, we consciously shift the emotions we experience, which naturally leads to more intentional actions and reactions. Intentional awareness of our thoughts allows us to break free from patterns that no longer serve us and to create a reality aligned with our higher vision.

BREATHING FOSTERS POSITIVE THOUGHTS

If our thoughts create our feelings, and our feelings shape our experience of the world, then *wouldn't it be imperative to be mindful of any thoughts we allow to take root in our minds?* When we focus on hopeful, kind, and empowering thoughts, we begin to feel those emotions and our world begins to shift accordingly.

To bring ourselves back to the center and ensure our thoughts are serving our highest good, one simple yet profoundly effective practice is the *4-7-8 breathing sequence* created by Dr. Andrew Weil. He recommends people use this style of breathing to fall asleep or go back to sleep when awoken at night. I have adapted this process of calm intentional breath for the purpose of activating more *magic*. This breathing technique is a powerful tool for calming the mind and creating space for more empowering, aligned thoughts to come through.

Using all three of these techniques—the 4-7-8 breathing sequence, intentional *what if* questions, and a focus on positive thoughts—can create a profound shift in your inner state. The 4-7-8 method calms your mind and body, creating the perfect space to introduce empowering *what if* questions, such as *'What if everything is working out for my highest good?'* or *'What if I am closer to my dreams than I realize?'*

As you breathe deeply and explore these expansive questions, your thoughts begin to align with the energy of possibility and *magic.* This process creates a sense of calm and clarity and encourages a powerful transformation in how you perceive and respond to the world. By combining these practices, you actively cultivate a mindset that attracts positivity, creativity, and alignment with your highest potential.

Here's how you can incorporate this practice into your life:

- First, gently breathe in through your nose for a count of four. Imagine drawing in peace, clarity, and grounding energy as you breathe in.
- Then, hold that breath for a count of seven. In this pause, your body naturally begins to settle, and you create spaciousness within yourself, allowing moments of stillness where worry can't reach.
- Finally, place your tongue on the space at the roof of your mouth behind your upper teeth, then exhale slowly through your nose for a count of eight, releasing all tension, fear, or chaotic thoughts cluttering your mind.

This practice is like hitting the reset button for your nervous system. When my mind is racing with worry or I feel overwhelmed, this simple breathwork helps bring me back into coherence. It gently quiets any noise and invites a deeper sense of peace, allowing awareness from a place of calm rather than reactivity. The beauty of the 4-7-8 breath is that it's always available as a tool to anchor yourself in the present moment and invite thoughts that nourish and uplift your spirit, no matter where you are or what's going on.

This technique isn't just about calming the mind; it's about creating a sacred space within yourself where you can *choose*, with intention, how you want to think, feel, and respond to life. It's a powerful reminder that we are always in control of our inner world, and with just a few mindful breaths, we can shift back to what matters most.

If you find your thoughts running rampant with fear, doubt, or over-whelm—pause and use your breath to calm yourself. The simple act brings you home, grounding you in the present moment. Once you've created that spaciousness, gently park the ego and tame your thoughts by focusing on something more expansive. From this place of calm, ask a powerful *what if* question. This question becomes the key to moving you forward, to breaking free from the confines of fear or limitation.

As you cultivate this practice, you'll begin to notice how new opportunities, insights, and solutions naturally arise. Each time you ask *what if,* you are not just seeking answers but opening the door to a fresh, new way of being. This will help you navigate life's challenges with grace and curiosity, turning what may have seemed like stumbling blocks into *stepping stones.* Trusting in the power of your breath, calming your thoughts, and asking the right questions naturally invite *magic* to flow into your life. The more you practice, the more you will realize that you hold the power to create the life you truly desire—one thought, one breath, one *what if* question at a time.

"What we think, we become."

BUDDHA

Chapter 5

Letting the False Fall Away

If you had met me in my teens, you would have seen a girl desperate for recognition and longing for public attention. By my twenties, I was focused on marriage and achieving the outward markers of success: the house, the cars, and the lifestyle that seemed to promise happiness. Something began to shift as I ventured through my thirties, forties, and fifties. I moved from wanting to accomplishing and from needing to truly experiencing. By my sixties and seventies, I found a stride that brought me the greatest peace and contentment. I allowed the false—the expectations, the illusions, and the facades—to fall away. What remained was a life that felt deeply authentic and beautifully aligned with who I truly am.

One of the most transformative steps on the journey to experiencing *magic* is learning to let the *false* fall away. This involves peeling back layers of old beliefs, attachments, and illusions that have built up over time. Old mental and emotional barriers prevent us from fully stepping into our authentic selves and living the expression of our true purpose. By releasing the 'unnecessary clutter' physically and emotionally, we make room for *magic* to flow without restraints. We return to the essence of who we are: unburdened, aligned, and free.

The process of letting go begins with refining our *discernment*—not just noticing disturbance on the surface but tuning in to how certain thoughts, emotions, and energies distract and impact us on a deeper level. A deeper meaning behind everything emerges if we ask ourselves: *What am I allowing into my inner sanctuary? What am I holding onto tightly? What is consuming my thoughts and emotions? What do I covet, and is it essential in my life?*

Deepening our inner truth can be the first step in allowing *magic* to appear. When we recognize what we hang onto or grasp to obtain, we often see what is getting in the way of what can truly fulfill us. For me, such clarity struck in a moment of deep crisis when everything felt like it was spiraling out of control. I found myself pacing the house, my heart pounding with fear, while my mind whirled with desperate questions: *What now? How do we survive these circumstances financially? What will we do to maintain our lifestyle? How will our lives be forced to change?* I felt rawness in that moment when everything felt exposed and dangerous. But within that urgency, I heard a faint whisper in the swirl of my desperation. I heard a deeper awareness and the call for 'voluntary simplicity.'

Unlike the chaos of my mind, that whisper carried a sense of peace and certainty. It did not offer answers in the traditional sense but rather a direction, a discerning need for *voluntary simplicity*, purging what no longer mattered. The Universe, in its infinite wisdom, was speaking to me. Not through thunderous signs but in a voice so subtle that it could only be heard when I *quieted my fears enough to listen*. I had to release what was holding me hostage in my *perceived* beliefs.

At first, I misunderstood the statement. I thought simplicity meant decluttering, organizing, or trimming away the physical distractions surrounding our lifestyle. But *voluntary simplicity* went far deeper than clearing away material things. The process was not about reducing the noise *around* me; it was about removing the noise *within me*. It was about letting go of everything that no longer served my highest good. The ideas, fears, expectations, and even relationships that no longer resonated with the deepest part of my heart needed to be released and purged from my life.

Stepping into *voluntary simplicity* was necessary for my evolution. It was a conscious, intentional command to surrender what no longer supported me and align with my soul's higher calling. 'Voluntary' meant I did it willingly, with grace, compassion, and trust. There was no resentment and no sense of loss. I only felt relief and the clarity that I would create space for something greater to emerge by freeing myself from old attachments.

'Simplicity' then became about creating an internal sanctuary—a space where only that which truly nourished my soul could remain. It was not about image, persona, or perfection but integral purity. It was about curating my inner world as an artist in a gallery, choosing only the most meaningful pieces to showcase. Each choice I made reflected my heart, truth, and highest values. Embarking on this task forced me to be *discerning* in every area of my life.

Through practice, I learned discernment means listening to the quiet, inner wisdom that guides us in recognizing what is essential and what no longer serves our greatest good. Tuning into our inner truth, we feel our way to differentiate between what nourishes us and that which drains us. Through discernment, we learn to recognize the frequencies that shape our experiences, understanding how certain thoughts, beliefs, and attachments either elevate or weigh us down. Discernment is not about judgment but about making conscious, compassionate choices to curate our inner refuge. We align with our soul's deepest desires by willingly releasing anything that does not support our growth. This process isn't about sacrifice; it's about empowerment. Discerning what truly belongs in our lives clears the path to fulfillment, purpose, and peace.

THE FREEDOM OF LETTING GO

As we venture more and more deeply into the beauty of voluntary simplicity, we realize that much of what we cling to—whether material possessions, beliefs, or even the need to control—stems from an internal fear. Fear that if we release certain things, we will somehow be less, have less, or miss out. But in truth, shedding emancipates us. It frees us to disengage from what no longer supports our evolution; it heartens our observation and reveals what truly matters, preparing us perfectly for our destined future.

Embracing voluntary simplicity invites us to seek deeper answers: *Does this serve my highest good? Does this expand me, or does it deplete me? Does this bring me joy or weigh me down?* When we engage with life in this way, we let go not out of obligation but out of love for ourselves, our growth, and our connection to something far greater. In such moments of discernment, we experience the *magic* of true alignment and freedom. We build a life where only what is meant *for* us remains, and all that no longer serves dissolves fluidly, with ease and dignity.

Letting go is not an act of loss; *it is an act of liberation*. It requires trust, self-love, and dedicated self-care to gift ourselves with freedom that is more aligned with who we truly are. When we step into a flow of life that allows *magic* to graciously appear, we create freely where rigidity once ruled. Letting go of any falseness is not about what we leave behind but what we make room for—a deeper connection to our purpose and the Divine wisdom within us.

My admired spiritual advisor, Pastor Steve, once offered the advice, "Give it all away—even your best things." His sentiment wasn't about charity in the material sense but about releasing the emotional, physical, and mental baggage that weighs us down. We can become slaves to our possessions, projects, and self-imposed obligations. But when we choose to let go of what no longer serves us, we create a new energy. We open the door to living a more carefree, 'gypsy-like' lifestyle, one that allows us to embrace the flow of life with lightness and playfulness.

Leaning more into our essence, the core of who we are, with the diminished need for external approval, we find we are enough *just as we are*. Things, accomplishments, and external validation will never fill us up. Only by being present in the world with the deep understanding that we are complete can we truly experience the *magic* we have within.

While writing this book, I reflected on the power of releasing and how deeply it has transformed my life. It inspired me to reach out to Pastor Steve, whose words profoundly influenced me at a pivotal time in my life. I asked if I could share his poem, which encourages deep trust in letting go, and he agreed. His poem, "Give it All Away," has had a lasting impact, offering me a perspective on surrender that *voluntary simplicity* conveys.

With Pastor Steve's permission, I'm delighted to share this profound poem with you. It perfectly portrays the power that comes from voluntary simplicity. His poem carries the essence of what I hope to convey in this book and my life: we don't diminish ourselves through release. Instead, we create space for the Divine, for *magic*, and for a richer, fuller life experience.

Give it all away
—Pastor Steve Garnaas-Holmes

Your stuff, your blessings,
your goodwill, your love.
Goodness, yes, your love.
Give away your best things,
your favorite things.
Don't hold back.
Pour it on, dump it out,
throw it all into people's laps.
Let everything good
flow like a spring from your river,
all of it—though it multiplies
as you surrender it.
Spend it, lose it, neglect it, waste it—
waste it on the least deserving,
the least understanding, the least aware.
Don't calculate as if you have to budget.

Ridiculously extravagant, fearlessly,
recklessly, giddily generous,
mindlessly raid your own savings of grace
and abandon it to your neighbors—
all your stuff, and God's as well,
until you have given it all away.

The crumbs of your love,
your pictures, your house, your floor,
the ground beneath you,
everything,
even your life
until there is nothing left
but God,

and you will be really alive.

MORE THAN JUST MATERIAL THINGS

As you can see, *voluntary simplicity* isn't just about decluttering your home or life; it's about creating *space* on every level—physically, emotionally, and spiritually. When we clear away things, relationships, and beliefs that no longer serve us, we open up to what truly matters. We are creating a haven in which we may thrive expansively.

"Everything false falls away," I remind myself and my cherished clients. This encouraging declaration begins to feel playful, sparking fresh curiosity to discover what expansiveness will show up when we drop the tired masks we wear, the identities and external appearances we've clung to, believing they define us or bring us happiness. Deep delight, which attracts the *magic* we seek, comes from living authentically, purely as our essence. Beyond clearing space, voluntary simplicity includes embracing the deep self. No longer focusing on the superficial and mundane, we free ourselves to stream as a fountain of energy into what truly lights us up. We virtually expand into passion and purpose for what gives our lives meaning and substance.

I once had a dream that spoke directly to this idea of identity and self. In the dream, I stood at the entrance of a cave. A wise Native American woman, adorned extravagantly in beads and fringes, handed me a jeweled dagger. With eyes full of ancient wisdom, she silently communicated that I was being called to release surface parts of myself—my attachment to appearances and identities I had outgrown. The message was clear: to live fully and authentically, I must vanquish the illusion that external success or outward appearances define my worth. I knew the dagger she handed me was a symbol of stripping away false parts of me that needed to fall from my life. No one else could do it but me. That dream helped me see wisdom and value in ending a masked existence and exiting a hiding place. It represented the deep inner work we all must do to drop our masks and be free.

Ultimately, letting go is an act of deep surrender. It requires listening within and trusting life's process, knowing that we don't need to control every outcome or have all the answers.

LETTING GO OF EGO AND ATTACHMENT

One of the greatest barriers to letting go is the 'False Self,' which thrives on insecurities, control, and a continual need for validation. It convinces us that if we cling to old identities, maintain appearances, or strive for perfection, we will be worthy, safe, or *in control*. Yet, these illusions of control are precisely what trap us in cycles of attachment and fear. The false self tells us we will lose something vital if we let go. But in truth, the opposite is often the case. As we learn to release the false self's grip, we step into a deeper space of authenticity, where freedom and growth await.

The false sense of control, or attachment to specific outcomes, often becomes an unconscious safety mechanism. We cling tightly to how we believe things *should* turn out, whether in relationships, careers, or other areas of life that matter to us. The false self wants certainty and security, so we fixate on achieving predictable results. We tell ourselves that if we hold on tightly enough, we can keep everything in line. But life is not meant to be controlled in such an erroneous way. When we try to force outcomes, we block the gift of *magic*, the potential for something more fulfilling and joyful than we could have imagined.

True freedom emerges when we surrender the need to control. Letting go of attachment to outcomes widens our receptivity to a much larger, Divine unfolding. In its infinite wisdom, the Universe will put forward plans that far surpass what we think we want. Surrendering to this greater plan is not an act of weakness; it's an act of profound trust that space is being cleared for *magic* to find you. We don't always get to know what lies ahead, but we can be certain that life is unfolding in our favor, even when we cannot see the whole picture beforehand.

Control can be seductive to our false selves by seemingly offering safety and certainty. On the surface, it feels like a shield that protects us from the chaos and unpredictability of life. Yet beneath this surface lies a more debilitating truth: control feeds off our darkest fears and insecurities. It draws its strength from the illusion that nothing can harm us if we just keep everything in check. This is the paradox of control: while it feels like a form of protection, it actually limits our growth and keeps us in a state of fear.

To transcend this dichotomy, we must honor the darkness within control and learn from it. The false self tells us to hold on, but the soul knows that true power lies in *release*. When we let go, we open ourselves to a more acceptable truth that embraces both the light and the dark. The dark beauty of control invites us to explore our shadows, confront the fears that keep us bound, and ultimately set them free. In doing so, we find that the very act of letting go creates space for healing, more *magic*, and a deeper connection to life itself.

THE 90-SECOND TECHNIQUE:
A PATH TO RELEASE

One of the most powerful tools I've discovered for letting go of attachment and control fuelled by the false self is the *ninety-second technique*, introduced by Dr. Jill Bolte Taylor in her book *My Stroke of Insight* and also explored in *Living Beautifully* by Pema Chödrön. This simple but transformative practice is based on the idea that any emotional response lasts only ninety seconds in the body unless we *choose* to prolong it by attaching a story or narrative to the emotion.

When a difficult or painful emotion arises—whether it's fear, anger, grief, or anxiety—the first instinct of the false self is to resist or control it. We either push the feeling away or try to rationalize it, trapping it within us where it can be triggered repeatedly. However, the ninety-second technique invites us to do the opposite: to sit with the emotion, to feel it fully, and to allow it to pass through us without judgment or resistance.

When you feel a surge of emotion, focus on the physical sensations it creates in your body. Do not distract yourself or attempt to 'fix' the emotion; simply feel it. Observe where the sensation is strongest. *Is it in your chest? Your throat? Your stomach?* Breathe deeply and magnify the feeling in your awareness. Stay with it for ninety seconds. As you do this, you may notice the intensity of the emotion begin to lessen. Within ninety seconds, it will naturally dissipate, like a wave washing through you.

The beauty of this technique is that it teaches us the impermanence of emotions we are willing to feel fully. No matter how intense a feeling may be in the moment, it cannot remain forever. By leaning into discomfort instead of avoiding it, we allow it to move through us and release it rather than letting it fester or control us.

This practice is particularly powerful when dealing with a perceived threat. Instead of tightening your grip on life, pause and permit yourself to experience the discomfort fully. When you allow the sensation of fear or uncertainty to run through your body without attaching a story to it, you voluntarily free yourself from its hold. You become the observer, watching the emotion rise and fall like a wave without being swept away by it.

The ninety-second technique helps us see that emotions, like everything else in life, are transient. They come and go. By embracing this truth, we develop the ability to release trapped emotions, knowing that even the most challenging feelings will pass if we simply allow them to. In letting go, we step into a space of voluntary surrender. We experience how life's beauty often lies in the unknown, in the spaciousness where we allow ourselves to be vulnerable and open. Control may feel safe, but true *magic*, the kind that transforms our lives, requires us to release our grip, trust in something greater, and know that whatever unfolds is leading us toward what will fuel our souls.

DARK BEAUTY IN THE EXTERNAL WORLD

My journey in life would not be complete if I did not have to face these falsities and confront my false self. Life has often presented me with external challenges that seem beyond my control. These experiences, whether illness, loss, or unforeseen obstacles, tested my spirit and affected my ability to surrender. I often speak of these moments as 'dark beauty' because life's darkest moments can undoubtedly carry the most potent gifts. External circumstances I could not control served to strip away the illusions I'd been holding onto. I had to shed the false layers of needing control to discover my true strength, my deepest truth, and a richer soulfulness that transcended all my fears.

When my husband Paul was battling cancer, we found ourselves immersed in the unknown, where control was utterly impossible. There were times when its weight felt crushing. But even in that darkness, light broke through. Moments of laughter, connection, and delight burst through the shadows and became the treasures we carried throughout the journey. Despite all the grief and darkness of those days, I learned the greatest lesson: *within every struggle, there is a seed of something beautiful waiting to be born.*

In moments of 'dark beauty,' internally and externally, we must allow the *false to fall away* in its entirety. We learn to trust that there is a Higher Purpose within the pain, uncertainty, and loss of control. This is the ultimate *dark beauty*; unknown gifts buried deep within suffering are orchestrated to guide us into new levels of self-awareness and wisdom.

When we release the attempt for false control, the path to our highest self is revealed in a blend between surrender and transformation. The term *dark beauty* speaks to how the most profound gifts in life are often liberated from our darkest passages. Through struggle, we are forced to confront the reality that there is little we can actually control. In times of vulnerability and uncertainty, we discover our true strength, resilience, and inner fortitude that transcends anything false. Life's challenges serve to remove the fictitious layers we have built around ourselves, revealing profound truths only adversity can unveil.

Dark beauty teaches us that not the absence of difficulty makes life beautiful but the way we embrace the interplay between the light and the dark. When we face external challenges, we are given the opportunity to let the false fall away. In these moments of voluntary surrender, we align with our highest self. We no longer cling to the need for control but learn to trust in the unfolding of life.

THE POWER OF THE SHINING MIRROR

Letting the false fall away is a human condition no different than learning to walk or develop a language. We all do it, go through it, and stumble along the way. As we navigate the internal and external challenges of being human, we often look to others as examples of what we are working toward. Along the way, we encounter people who inspire us with their light, joy, strength, and pure presence. These individuals serve as mirrors, reflecting qualities we already possess within ourselves, even if we don't fully recognize them yet.

When we admire someone's courage, creativity, or kindness, it's because these traits are already present within us and available to be nurtured. I call these people 'Shining Mirrors' because they reflect what exists inside us, revealing what we are capable of becoming. These individuals represent what we value and act in ways we're drawn to because we recognize their gifts within ourselves. Noticing them as mirrors reminds us that we are not separate from the qualities we admire in others; they are essential pieces of our own being.

As we observe these qualities in people around us, we begin to understand they are not foreign or unreachable. These shining mirrors are powerful reminders of the potential we carry within ourselves. The light we admire in others reflects the qualities we are ready to embrace but have not fully acknowledged. By observing them, we receive both inspiration and validation that we are on the right path. We see fresh possibilities within our own growth, showing us what is available when we move beyond limitations and self-doubt.

Each encounter with a shining mirror encourages us to peel back layers of apprehension, revealing more of our authentic selves. The more we recognize and foster these qualities, the brighter our own light becomes, empowering us to serve as shining mirrors for others along their path.

The Shining Mirror Exercise

- Try the *shining mirror exercise* to deepen your awareness of recognizing your gift to others. Begin by reflecting on someone who embodies qualities that light you up—whether it's their honesty, resilience, or humility. Write down the specific traits you admire in them.
- Then, take a moment to acknowledge that these qualities are not only in the person you respect but also within you.
- Next, consider how you might cultivate these traits in your own life. For example, if you admire someone's tenacity, ask yourself where you have shown tenacity in your own life. If you admire someone's compassion, reflect on the ways you already express compassion to yourself or others.
- The shining mirror reveals traits we see in others as a reflection of the traits that await nurturance within ourselves.

As you practice this exercise, you'll notice that as you let go of the false—the need for external validation, control, or attachment—these radiant qualities within you shine even brighter. This is the power of the shining mirror: it reflects the beauty in others and reveals your own inner light to you.

I also invite you to create a list of people you aspire to emulate. In making this list, you begin to understand that the qualities you admire reflect your potential waiting to be activated. As you identify these traits, ask yourself: *How can I nurture these qualities in my own life? Where have I already displayed them, even if in small ways?* This conscious self-reflection helps you shift from passive admiration to active development.

Identifying and cultivating the traits you appreciate is a powerful form of instilling *magic.* It shifts your mindset from seeing those qualities as something others have and you lack to recognizing them as part of your own internal makeup. The more you engage with this exercise, the more you will see how interconnected we are. Just as you observe exceptional qualities in others, others see them in you. When you nurture your own abilities, you naturally become a *shining mirror* for those around you. You inspire others to recognize their potential, creating a ripple effect of growth, evolution, and empowerment.

As you continue to develop these innate qualities, pay attention to how your relationships and interactions begin to shift. The more you embody traits you admire, the more you attract people and opportunities that align with your true self. This is the essence of expecting *magic!*

Here's to the beauty of *shining mirrors*—they show us what is possible and so much more about who we are at our core. They lead us to embrace more of the *magic* available and let the rest, the false, fall away.

Remember, the false self is merely a mask, not a reflection of who you truly are. Peeling away layers helps uncover the truth about who you are destined to become. The more you express your real self, the more you will experience the *magic* of what you and the Universe can co-create.

"Thou shalt acknowledge the wonder."

—D. LAWRENCE

Chapter 6

Embracing Change
with Grace

If you picked up this book looking for one golden nugget of wisdom from me or one profound concept that would shift the trajectory of your life, then let me share that one constant truth I have held: *Change is inevitable in life.* And how we embrace that change, with grace, openness, and curiosity, determines the quality of our journey going forward.

In the last chapter, I spoke about how true transformation begins when we are willing to *release attachments* that no longer serve us and open ourselves to the voluntary simplicity that will free us. In these moments of surrender, *magic* filters into our lives in unexpected and serendipitous ways. Yet, it is in the grace and willingness to welcome such change that we activate the *magic* we seek.

That said, not everyone finds change easy. In fact, change often feels so unsettling and worrisome that it stirs up resistance within us. It's natural to experience hesitation and resistance when life asks us to evolve. But resistance is simply a sign that you are on the edge of something new, something that has the potential to expand you. By acknowledging the apprehension or discomfort and still *choosing* to move forward with curiosity, you can transform that resistance into a stepping stone for growth. When you embrace change, even with uncertainty, you allow new opportunities to unfold, options that wouldn't have been available if you had stayed in the familiar. Change becomes less of a burden and more of an invitation to step into the *magic* waiting for you.

Embracing change involves aligning ourselves with our deepest desires and trusting that our future will meet us halfway. It's a co-creation between action and surrender, between holding a vision and allowing life to unfold in its own time. I've seen this in my own life and countless clients who have stepped beyond their comfort zones and into their power by embracing new circumstances. I have witnessed people shift from complication to clarity, hesitancy to contentment. Change means progressing from one emotion, situation, or circumstance to another. We can also influence how that change unfolds and how we feel about it.

There is a wonderful quote by Joseph Campbell: "The cave you fear to enter holds the treasure you seek." It reminds me that within every experience lies the potential for something transformative. The losses, setbacks, and moments of grief are not obstacles but gateways to something even greater. They hold buried treasures that can lead us to a richer, more textured life. When we embrace them with the desire *for* change, we invite change in. We shift our perspective and enliven something magical.

Instead of resisting change, we can ask ourselves, *What richness may I discover from this? What hidden treasures await me on the other side of this experience?* Or, even more playfully, *How can I learn to boogie in the void?* Simply making inquiries, even silly ones, permits us to move beyond any constriction and into a space of newness and transformation.

LIVING WITH PURPOSE AND PASSION

Living a life with purpose and passion requires us to change, not sit idle or wait for it to happen, but to invite change in. Not everyone is comfortable with asking for change to transpire. Change can feel daunting, especially when it disrupts the patterns and routines we've grown accustomed to. The unknown can feel like a blank canvas, void of structure or familiarity, and for many, that can stir anxiety and resistance. In these moments, we're faced with a choice: cling to the safety of the familiar or welcome the momentary discomfort to let the *magic* occur.

One of the most powerful techniques I teach for moving through these feelings and embracing change is to view your life as a work of art. Every experience, both joyful and painful, becomes a brush-stroke on the canvas of your life. The masterpiece of your existence takes shape in the contrast between light and dark, joy and sorrow. When you begin to see your life this way, you start to appreciate the richness changes bring, even the difficult ones.

There is a concept in art known as 'chiaroscuro,' which comes from the Italian words *chiaro*, meaning 'light,' and *scuro*, meaning 'dark.' This technique refers to the contrast between light and shadow, a method artists like Caravaggio and Rembrandt mastered to create depth, emotion, and intensity in their work. Through this interplay of light and darkness, a painting comes to life, revealing its true power and beauty.

But *chiaroscuro* is not just a concept reserved for art. It reflects the human experience. The most profound beauty emerges in the contrast between our struggles and triumphs, our darkest moments, and our most brilliant successes. Without the presence of darkness, light lacks depth and significance. Our glorious and victorious moments wouldn't hold the same meaning without their challenges.

Often, we fear the dark moments in life, those periods of uncertainty, pain, or failure. Yet, by remembering to open and move into these moments, we *feel* our way into our greatest opportunities for growth *and* change. Just as an artist uses shadow to expose the brilliance of light, our struggles deepen our capacity for wisdom, resilience, and happiness. We emerge transformed each time we encourage ourselves to move through the darkness.

Think about your own life. Reflect on times when things felt like they were falling apart, only for you to emerge stronger and more connected to your true self. This is *chiaroscuro* at play. The contrast of life's challenges and triumphs reveals the increased fullness of your experience. You enriched the canvas of your life, giving it texture and depth that wouldn't exist otherwise.

Chiaroscuro reminds us that life, like art, is shaped by contrast that precedes change. Difficult moments, while uncomfortable, are essential to activate the change we need. They give meaning to the light-filled moments that follow and facilitate *magic* to preside.

The key to navigating *chiaroscuro* is to be on purpose and stay curious. Ask yourself the important questions: *What more is here for me at the moment? What am I meant to learn? How can I soothe and embrace my feelings? What magic will appear from this?* Often, we are so focused on what we *think* we should do or how we should be that we forget to listen to that inner voice guiding us toward our true purpose. We resist and contract; we scramble in the dark when we are meant to expand and rejoice in the light that always exists.

Your life is a work of art! Every experience, opportunity, and circumstance filled with excitement or sorrow is part of the masterpiece. The contrast between the dark shadows and the illuminated light gives your life magnificent depth and profound meaning. By widening your perception of the totality of your experience, you see how your most challenging moments shape you into becoming the person you were created to be.

GRACE IN THE FACE OF CHANGE

One of the most valuable lessons I've learned in my own *chiaroscuro* of life is to pause and welcome change with grace. Grace is the soulful essence that allows us to surrender into the unknown, to trust that even amid chaos, there is beauty to be found. When Paul was nearing the end of his life, an incredible sense of peace came over us. We stopped running from the truth, and in that acceptance, we found moments of joy, love, and connection that transcended the pain. Of course, his passing felt dark and stormy, but in that contrast, we found light. I remember us reminiscing over past trips and recalling memories of both beautiful *and* challenging times. With him nearing the end, we uncovered ways to laugh about insignificant things and let go of everything that no longer mattered. As Paul was parting, I chose to no longer rage against the injustice or the grief; I decided to be in the frequency of grace, peace, and reverence for our time together and the tremendous gifts of Divine grace he bestowed.

Grace is not something that comes easily, especially in the face of difficulties. We have to cultivate it, inviting it into our lives by being fully present through times of illumination and darkness. We must look for grace in ourselves and others, practice benevolence in our daily interactions, and trust that a softer, kinder way is available.

When we ask *how we can invite grace into this experience*, we open floodgates of grace to pour in. Simply asking invites its arrival and opens ways for it to smooth the edges of what life brings. Grace appears through acknowledging the messiness of life and accepting that we don't have all the answers. It softens us to be okay with not knowing, to trust life, and to notice that beauty has begun to brighten what is yet to be revealed.

CONNECTING WITH YOUR INNER GRACE

In those moments when we require grace, turning inward is a powerful way to calm our thoughts. By choosing to focus introspectively, we create a space of stillness where we are attuned to our inner wisdom, listening to the voice within that fosters grace. This is where the practice of self-reflection through journaling becomes a sacred tool. It leads us to tap into that inner knowing, a form of self-awareness, and a deeper conversation with ourselves.

Journaling is one of the most powerful tools we have for tapping into inner knowing. Engaging in conversation with our Higher Selves we explore our desires, fears, and hopes. When we journal, we permit ourselves to be honest and raw, to express what we might be afraid to say aloud. It's in those moments of honesty that we find clarity.

There's something profoundly healing in self-honesty. Unguarded moments allow clarity in which we can untangle the complexities of our emotions and find a path forward.

During the four months of Paul's decline from cancer, journaling became my lifeline. I had so many emotions that I didn't know how to release. In his quiet strength, Paul asked me to stay cheerful and keep his illness private. I honored his wishes, but it meant that I carried alone a deep well of grief, anger, and fear that had no outlet. Journaling became my refuge. It was where I could pour out the feelings I couldn't share with anyone. Each time I wrote, it felt like I was conversing with not only Paul's eternal self but with the Divine, speaking my truth and being heard in a way that nothing else allowed. I told myself, "Feelings are fleeting," but only if they are honored and processed.

After he passed, amid my grief, I began writing questions to myself: *What is possible for me now? What might the whole new chapter of my life reveal? What whole new opportunity do I truly want to create?* These questions became doorways, shifting my focus from loss to hope. Even in the depths of sorrow, a promise of a future *I could still shape* appeared. Journaling those answers moved me beyond the heaviness of my sorrow, transforming pain into a fresher sense of who I might become.

Over time, my journaling practice has evolved into many volumes that have guided me forward, lifted me up, and walked me through my many life passages. My journaling has become more than just a practice of reflection; it has been a haven for deepening the messages meant specifically for me. Over time, my journaling practice grew into an ongoing relationship with my Higher Self and the Divine, and I began using *Divine Dialogues* to help me through.

When we journal, we create space for our souls to speak freely. It's a practice of releasing what weighs us down while discovering the hidden promise within the answers we've been searching for. Through honest dialogue with ourselves and the Divine, we gradually heal and open to the grace that will guide us toward our next steps. As change becomes inevitable, our journal and the dialogue they foster create a constant source of reassurance.

DIVINE DIALOGUE & JOURNALING

When your thoughts lead to confusion, turn to your journal. Let it be the place where you listen to your heart and invite your inner wisdom to lead you forward. *Self-reflective questions*, inspired by change, open a portal to messages we need to hear. They create private space for poignant and meaningful conversation with the Divine, our Higher Selves conferring with the Creator of all things.

Each time we reflect and look inward, we awaken to new possibilities and open ourselves to Divine guidance. Through introspection and openness, we invite the Universe to respond and whisper answers into the quiet spaces we've opened through inquiry. From that place of self-inquisitiveness and vulnerable introspection, we can move from indecision into conviction, from feeling stuck to feeling guided. By utilizing *Divine Dialogue* in these moments of deep inner truth, you can access an ongoing conversation with the expansiveness of all that is forever available to us when we are willing to listen.

In sacred dialogue, we are not alone. We communicate with a Higher Source of wisdom, whether you call it God, Spirit, or the energy of the Source itself. Where do the answers and the sudden clarity come from? Some say it is the subconscious mind—our inborn servant that slaves diligently to solve problems. Some say angels are standing by, but they won't act unless we ask.

What really matters is that the process works. We become both the speaker and the listener, engaging in a sacred unity with the Divine. In these moments of inner reflection, we receive the insights we need, the gentle nudges that remind us we are supported and that our path is unfolding exactly as it should.

The practice of *Divine Dialogue* taps into limitless wisdom and trust that we are always being guided toward our highest good, even when we can't yet see the full picture. It's connecting with Higher Wisdom, the Collective Consciousness, or what physicists might call the Unified Field. Here is where all answers live, the source of knowledge far greater than ourselves. When we engage in Divine Dialogue, we are open to the universe's *magic* communicating with us.

Asking with inquisitiveness and vulnerability helps activate the *magic* within such sacred conversation and infuses us with an inner knowing gracefully designed to guide us. The Universe, in its infinite wisdom, is always listening, encouraging, and ready to support us when we take the time to connect with it. I encourage you to trust in the process and find how, through *Divine Dialogue*, you are receiving gifts of grace and love you have within yourself.

HOW TO USE *DIVINE DIALOGUE WHEN JOURNALING*

Engaging in *Divine Dialogue* is a powerful way to connect with your own inner wisdom and the Divine. It's a practice of both journaling and dialoguing that provides insights, clarity, and guidance while helping you process your thoughts and emotions. Here's how you can begin this transformative practice:

1. Create a Sacred Space

Find a quiet, comfortable space to be safely alone with your thoughts. Light a candle, play soft music, or do whatever helps you feel grounded and connected. This is a private time to center yourself and set the intention of enjoying a meaningful conversation.

2. Calm Your Mind with a Breath

Before you begin journaling, take a few deep breaths. Close your eyes, and let your breathing slow down. Use the 4-7-8 breath technique (inhale for four counts, hold for seven, and exhale for eight) to quiet your mind and bring yourself into a state of calm presence. This helps clear mental clutter and opens you to receive the guidance waiting for you.

3. Creating an Opening Statement for Divine Dialogue

Before you begin your journaling session, take a moment to center yourself. Consider it setting the stage for a conversation with your Higher Self. Begin by asking *What am I seeking clarity on?*

What insight would I love to receive today? What do I need to learn that will serve my highest good?

Write down whatever comes to mind as the foundation of your inquiry. Your opening statement doesn't have to be complex or elaborate—just a clear expression of what you're inviting into sacred dialogue.

By writing down an opening statement, you signal to the universe and yourself that you are ready to receive answers. This simple practice helps ground your journaling session in intention, making it easier for the *magic* of Divine Dialogue to unfold.

4. Ask Yourself a *what if* Question

Expand your journaling inquiry by asking an open-ended *What If* question. This question is key to shifting your mindset from feeling stuck or overwhelmed to one of curiosity and possibility. For example:

- *What if there is another way to approach this situation?*
- *What if I'm exactly where I need to be right now?*
- *What if this challenge is leading me to something greater?*

Allow these questions to guide the flow of your thoughts.

5. Listen to the Whisper of the Divine

As you journal, know that you're tapping into and engaging in a dialogue with unlimited Source. Write down whatever comes to you without judgment or overthinking. This is not about getting the right answers or judging what comes through but letting the messages flow freely. Allow your thoughts to unfold naturally, trusting that the insights you receive are coming from a deeper source of wisdom.

6. Be Both the Speaker and the Listener

As you write, think of yourself as both the one asking and the one receiving answers. You're speaking to the Divine, but you're also listening to what is being shared back to you. This process of journaling becomes a sacred conversation where you are simultaneously expressing yourself and tuning into Higher Guidance.

7. Allow for Silence and Reflection

Once you've written down your thoughts, pause. Sit with what you've written, allowing space for the deeper messages to settle. Sometimes, the answers don't come immediately, and that's okay. Trust that the clarity you seek will reveal itself in time.

8. Ask for Guidance in Specific Areas

If you feel stuck in a particular area of your life, ask for guidance in that specific situation. For example:

- *What if I let go of this fear?*
- *What if I'm ready for the next step in my journey?*
- *What if I embrace what I am resisting?*

Be specific in your questions, and let the answers flow through you as you journal. The Divine always responds when we ask with openness.

9. End with Gratitude

When you feel your journaling session is complete, take a moment to express gratitude. Thank the Divine, the Universe, or your Higher Self for the insights and guidance you've received. This seals the practice with appreciation and signals that you are ready to receive whatever unfolds next in your journey.

10. Trust in the Process

By incorporating *Divine Dialogue* into your daily journaling practice, you cultivate a deeper connection with your own inner wisdom. Utilizing ongoing conversation will help you navigate life's challenges with more clarity, peace, and trust. Over time, you'll learn how the answers you seek are always within reach, waiting for you to listen and act from a place of Divine alignment.

Divine Dialogue is a practice of trust. The answers you need come at the right time and in the right way. Sometimes, insights are immediate; other times, they will appear unexpectedly throughout your day or week. As you continue journaling, you keep the conversation flowing and invite the messages to come more frequently.

ILLUMINATED JOURNALS:
PRESERVING THE JOURNEY

If you want to take your journaling practice in a more artful direction, as a joyful legacy project, consider a special version that I call 'Illuminated Journals.' These journals were not just a record of emotions and events but a way of capturing the essence and *magic* of life. I love to carry colorful pens, stickers, and a bound notebook with me everywhere, documenting family moments, road trips, special occasions, and inspired feelings we all spontaneously encounter. I write the appreciations and experiences of the moment and later print out and paste in photos to accompany the words, creating a visual and emotional tapestry of my life.

These journals have become cherished treasures for me and my family. They hold the stories, feelings, and memories that might otherwise be forgotten. Over time, they became so precious that my family insisted they be kept in a special box near the front of the garage so they could be saved if there was ever a fire. These journals are not just books; they reflect the journey I have been on, the joys and sorrows I have experienced, and the deep sense of *homecoming* I continually discover along the way.

Looking back through these journals, I see how far I've come. I love to revisit recorded moments of beauty, challenge, and growth to gain new perspectives on the path that has led me here. Ten years from now, when I open one of these journals, I will sense even more meaning in my recorded experiences. This is the value of illuminated journals—they are a way to preserve for ourselves and future generations our artfully illustrated experiences. They reveal our rich and meaningful life journey.

YOUR DIVINE CONNECTION

To close this chapter, I invite you to sit with the truth that your life is not just happening to you—it is unfolding *through* you, shaped by every choice, every moment of surrender, every brushstroke of light and shadow. Embracing change with intentionality is an act of trusting your masterpiece in progress. The more we allow ourselves to flow in the rhythm of life, the more we open to the *magic* of transformation.

Each challenge is a passage, each joy a gift, and each moment an opportunity to deepen our connection with divinity and grace. The treasures of transformation lie waiting for us to step into the *magic* of life unfolding moment by moment, thought by thought, breath by breath.

> *"And the day came when the risk to remain tight in a bud was more painful than the risk it took to blossom."*
>
> —ANAÏS NIN

Chapter 7

The Heart of Homecoming

Until now, I have shared a lot about the experiences we create, the connections we form, and the actions we must take to awaken the *magic* we so divinely have access to. I have talked about frequency, reflection, awakening, and letting the false fall away to evoke a deeper connection with the *magic* we seek. I have also given tips, insights, and many techniques to stir and stimulate the *magic* that surrounds us—the essence of what is possible in our lives.

For much of life, before we uncover these truths, we are seekers blindly searching for a way to piece together the puzzle of existence. Yet the moment we feel that *magic*, recognize its presence, and experience its power, we connect with a part of ourselves that has always been whole. This is the feeling of returning home to yourself, of solving a conundrum that was uniquely yours to unravel. It is the profound realization of rediscovering and treasuring that most sacred place within.

If you are unsure what the *Heart of Homecoming* means, imagine a weary traveler who has spent years wandering through dense forests, crossing endless deserts, and scaling rugged mountains, all in search of a treasure they believe will finally bring them the happiness and fulfillment they long for. Along the way, the traveler gathers maps and advice from others, filling their pack with tools and trinkets, each hopeful to unlock the secret to the treasure's location. The journey is long, and with every step, the traveler believes that the answer awaits just beyond the next horizon.

But as the years pass, the excitement fades. The weight of the journey feels heavier. The once clear anticipation of the treasure grows hazy, lost in the endless pursuit. Exhaustion settles in, and one day, the traveler finds oneself in a quiet, sunlit clearing. Tired, they set down their heavy pack and sit on the soft earth, allowing one to rest for the first time in a long while.

In the stillness of that moment, something shifts. The traveler notices not the world around them but the harsh ambition of their wanderlust. They feel the weight they've carried, the striving, the endless search without results. Amidst the retrospection, something inside starts to soften. A sense of peace begins to rise from within, and with it, a deep gratitude for the *journey*, not for where it led, but for how it shaped them. They newly sense the richness of their inner quest, the strength they never acknowledged, and the quiet wisdom that was always there, patiently waiting to be welcomed.

In such stillness, the traveler realizes the treasure was never hidden in some distant place. It was buried in their own heart all along—suppressed beneath layers of doubt, disappointment, and the constant striving for more. What they had been seeking was already within: an *inner sanctum* awaiting stillness to reveal. The treasure was never external; it was their abiding inner wholeness, quiet knowing, and innate beauty, patiently waiting for them to return *home*.

This is the heart of Homecoming, the moment when we realize that all the fulfillment and contentment we have been chasing isn't something to be found outside of ourselves. It's the return to a deep knowing that has always been *within* us, waiting for us to pause, be still, listen, and receive.

Homecoming isn't about reaching for more or achieving something new. It's about releasing the demands we've carried for so long, dispersing the expectations, the judgments, and the fears that have kept us disconnected from our true selves. The *magic* of coming home to self is a gentle process of softening until the simple, beautiful truth remains that we are truly enough, just as we are. Allowing those layers of false desires to fall away, we rediscover the peace and contentment that have always been within us, quietly calling us back home to ourselves, revealing the *magic* we possessed all along.

THE JOURNEY OF SELF-DISCOVERY AND HEALING

The process of Homecoming is not about searching for *more* in our lives. It is about stripping away the layers of *anticipation*, *need*, and *want* that cloud our essence. Allowing these layers to fall away, we hear the inner knowing of our soul calling us back home. At home, at last, we feel a deep sense of safety and contentment, where there is no need to strive because we realize that everything we need is already within. We can confront the external illusions we've held onto and release the ideas, beliefs, and attachments that have kept us from fully embracing who we are.

Most people believe they want something external, such as more money, a better job, or a perfect relationship, but they are truly seeking a feeling that attainment will provide. When we come home to ourselves, we seek not to find but to *feel*. We desire deeper, more fulfilling sensations and the *magic* of life itself. Beyond attainment and accumulation, we *choose* to feel safe, nurtured, and complete. We aspire to have that internal *knowledge* above all else.

There is an exercise I love to share that helps people connect with a deeper truth about themselves. It begins with a simple inquiry: *What do I truly want?* At first, the answer might seem obvious or surface-level, things like success, security, or recognition. But this is where the real work begins. Once you have an answer the first time, inquire again: *And if I had that, then what do I want?* This practice of inquiring is not meant to be rushed; it's a journey into the layers of your desires. The initial answer is rarely the deepest truth.

Inquire repeatedly, peeling back each layer of what you think you want. Each time you answer, you dig deeper, uncovering the motivations and emotions beneath your initial response. With each iteration, *What do I want if I had that?*—you move closer to your core. Eventually, you realize that the things you *thought* you wanted were not the root of your desire. They were placeholders for something more profoundly internal.

The repetition of this inquiry reveals that what we truly seek is not external. It's not about attainments, possessions, or praise from others. Instead, we deeply crave a sense of *Homecoming*, to feel the welcome of being at home in our own skin, experiencing peace, groundedness, and fullness that doesn't depend on anything outside of us.

When you inquire enough times, you start to see that you want to experience wholeness, to be connected to yourself on the most authentic level. The need for external validation or material success falls away, leaving you with the purity of feeling complete and at ease within your own being. This exercise is not just about finding answers; it's about stripping away the distractions, the masks, and the false narratives we've been living by. It's about finding the truth beneath the layers, the truth always waiting for you.

As you continue to ask, *And if I had that, then what do I want?*, you create space for deeper clarity. The process may take time, and it might feel uncomfortable as you let go of the things you thought mattered. But in the end, you realize that all you've ever wanted is to feel at peace with yourself, feel a sense of belonging within, a connection to your heart, and trust your place in the world.

This practice of asking these questions is powerful because it reminds us that the answers are not *out there*. They are already within us, waiting to be bared. The more you uncover the layers, the closer you come to that sense of inner homecoming. That is the magical place where you feel whole, enough, and deeply connected to your pure essence.

I remember that pivotal moment when Paul and I attended a workshop where, for the first time, we were asked the question: *What do you really want?* At the start, our answers were predictable. We wanted things like success, recognition, and love, things that seemed like the keys to happiness. But as we continued to ask the question and dig deeper, we realized that what we truly wanted was something far more profound. We wanted to feel at home within ourselves and with each other. It wasn't about the external; it was about *shared love*, inner peace, and the quiet contentment that comes from truly being received and accepted.

At that moment, I crawled into Paul's lap, and we both wept. We understood that our deepest desire wasn't tied to any achievement or external marker of success. It was about feeling welcome within ourselves and with each other. This was our Homecoming—a return to the heart of who we are, where we could rest in love and belonging. It was our sacred knowing that the greatest homecoming as a couple was to be truly received as our individual and sacred selves.

THE GIFT OF HOMECOMING

Ultimately, what we all seek is to feel at home within ourselves. Whether we have a partner or not, the most valuable relationship we can cultivate is the one we have with ourselves. When we feel safe and nurtured by our own being, we can move through life with ease, grace, and contentment.

I experienced this feeling of coming fully home to myself profoundly after my second husband, Ted, passed away. Having been married to two wonderful men for a total of 56 years—first Paul and then Ted—I found myself standing at the threshold of a whole new life. Beneath the grief and loss of losing my second beloved husband, there was buried treasure—a liberating sense of sovereignty and Homecoming to *my* essence. For the first time, I had boundless space to explore who I was on my own terms. I no longer needed to accommodate the needs of others; I didn't need to be a wife, companion, or lover. Instead, I could pour my energy into nurturing and expanding my soul, my gifts, and the innermost essence of who I could become.

That was a time of profound transformation, awakening to *my* sovereignty. I learned to live in continual 'Divine Dialogue,' asking profound questions and trusting the 'Dark Beauty' to reveal answers. I moved at my own pace, listened to my inner voice, and allowed myself to be fully present with my emotions. While the pain of loss was real, there was also a comforting sense of peace and Homecoming that carried me through.

When we come home to ourselves, we no longer seek from the outside world. We recognize that everything we need is available within us, and from this place of fullness, we can give freely and receive gracefully. We become fountains, pouring our love, purpose, and gifts into the world without fear of depletion. This is the true *magic* of Homecoming: returning to the truth of who we are, embracing our wholeness, and sharing our uniqueness with the world. Evolving from this new spaciousness, we can create lives filled with meaning and purpose. We move through the world with elegance and gratitude, knowing we are always supported, always enough, and always at home.

When we move from seeking to *feeling*—into fullness, wholeness, alignment, and truth—we become more connected and present in our lives. These qualities anchor us deeply, allowing us to experience life from a place of alignment and confidence. Embodying such feelings helps us see what it truly means to come home to ourselves and live in harmony with who we are at the core of our being.

HOMECOMING INCLUDES THE HEART

When you think about homecoming in your life, focus on the emotions you most desire to feel. Place your hand on your heart, the center of your emotions, close your eyes, and consciously bring forth what it needs to thrive. Your heart is the foundation that brings you into coherence and presence. It serves as the epicenter of what defines *home within you.* Allow these important feelings to infuse everything you do and guide how you experience your day. Make space for them, ensure they are felt deeply, and let your actions reflect and nurture them. In doing so, you create a life that feels truly aligned with the essence of what it means to be you. This alignment opens the doorway to the emotions we all deeply desire to feel and is the foundation of the homecoming we seek within ourselves.

As we explore this heart-centered homecoming, let's focus on four core emotions that define this sense of coming home: *fullness, wholeness, alignment,* and *truth.* These primary feelings bring us closer to the *magic* of who we are and allow us to appreciate every aspect of our lives. The journey to embody these emotions is an invitation to come home to one's self, rediscover the essence of who you are, and live a beautiful and complete life.

Let's explore what it means to welcome fullness, wholeness, alignment, and truth into your life—and how you can infuse these feelings into your life right now.

Fullness:

Fullness is the sense of being content without the need for more. It is an acceptance that we already have everything we need. When we feel full, we do not chase external validation or material success. Instead, we recognize the richness of our inner landscape. Fullness comes from embracing all aspects of ourselves, both the light and the shadow, and knowing that we are enough, just as we are.

- **Practice Gratitude:** Begin or end each day by listing three things you're grateful for, focusing on what you already have in your life. This shifts your attention from lack to abundance.
- **Savor Simple Moments:** When you eat, walk, or engage in daily routines, slow down and fully immerse yourself in the experience. Notice the richness of the moment.
- **Affirm Sufficiency:** Repeat affirmations like "I know I am enough" or "I have everything I need within me" throughout the day to reinforce a sense of internal completeness.

Wholeness:

Wholeness is the state of being integrated and unified within ourselves. It means accepting every part of our being, past, emotions, and experiences and allowing them to coexist without judgment. Wholeness is not about being perfect or flawless. By embracing the entirety of who we are, we accept how each part serves a purpose in our journey. When we feel whole, we are at peace with our complexities and stand strong in our authenticity.

- **Embrace Your Story:** Reflect on the parts of your past or personality you may have resisted. Write down how each of these aspects has helped shape who you are today.
- **Body Awareness:** Spend a few minutes each day placing your hands over your heart and taking slow, deep breaths. As you do, silently affirm, "Every part of me feels at home."
- **Visual Integration:** Imagine gathering fragments of yourself, your emotions, memories, and experiences and gently bringing them together into a unified whole. Picture yourself feeling peaceful and complete.

Alignment:

Alignment is the harmony between our inner truth and how we live our lives. Our actions, choices, and intentions align with our highest values and desires. When we are aligned, there is no internal conflict or dissonance. Instead, we feel guided by a deep sense of purpose and clarity. Living in alignment, we trust ourselves and our path, sensing Divine direction that is true to our soul.

- **Values Check-In:** Write down your top three core values and reflect on whether your current actions align with them. If not, adjust your focus or commitments to realign.
- **Set Daily Intentions:** Before starting your day, identify one action that will bring you closer to living in harmony with your inner truth.
- **Listen to Your Intuition:** Practice tuning into your intuition by pausing before making decisions. Do your *Divine Dialogue* practice to decide, "Does this feel right for me?" and trust the answer that arises.

Truth:

Truth is the steadfast inner knowing that arises when we strip away the layers of illusion and fear. It is the clarity we find behind false narratives we've been living by and in direct contact with our authentic selves. Truth doesn't change with external circumstances; it remains steady and unwavering. When we live in truth, we feel grounded and empowered, no longer swayed by the opinions or expectations of others. Truth is the foundation of our inner home-coming; when we stand in it, we experience the freedom of being fully ourselves.

- **Quiet the Noise:** Spend time in silence or meditation daily to connect with your inner voice. This practice helps you differentiate between external influences and your authentic self.

- **Question Narratives:** Notice the stories you tell yourself about who you are or what you 'should' do. Challenge any that feel limiting or untrue, and reframe them with more empowering truths.
- **Speak Honestly:** Practice expressing your truth in small ways, like sharing your feelings with someone you trust or writing a letter to yourself about what matters most to you.

As we welcome and cultivate these feelings, we bring balance and cohesive order to all we do. This fosters the felt sense of homecoming and allows more solidity in how we show up and progress. All of life is an evolution, and these feelings bring that to a heart-centered place where *magic* happily enriches us to feel and experience even more.

SUPPORTING OUR EVOLUTION

Despite being in my twilight years, I still have what it takes to use and appreciate today's technology. Coming home to oneself is an inside job, but that doesn't mean we can't utilize the latest science and research available to make 'coming home' even more accessible.

The most powerful tool I've found for empowering and reconnecting with myself is NuCalm™. It's an app on my phone and iPad that I deeply enjoy using, and it has become an essential part of my daily practice of feeling at home and at peace. I want to share this with you because sometimes we can benefit greatly from tools and support that allow us to feel a deeper connection with the essence of ourselves. NuCalm uses advanced science—through gentle sounds carried via headphones—to slow down our brainwaves, guiding them into a deeply restorative state called *theta*. This is the same state just before deep sleep, where your body heals, your cells detoxify, and your entire being feels a profound sense of calm.

I use NuCalm to begin my day or to pause and reset. I put on my headphones and let the soothing music carry me away. The *magic* of this experience is that I don't have to control anything. The breath of life flows through me, slowing my mind and body down. After about thirty or forty minutes, I feel refreshed, peaceful, and deeply connected to my core. It's as if I've unplugged from the external noise and plugged directly into the source of my inner effervescence and vitality.

NuCalm allows me to access that sense of *Homecoming*—the deep resonance within that we all long for. In a world where we're often running on autopilot, living in a constant state of hyper-vigilance, NuCalm helps me shift out of fight-or-flight mode and back into a state of being. It's like sitting on a beach, hearing the waves, feeling at one with nature, and sensing that everything in life is beautifully connected. It brings me back to my spirit, reminding me of my connection to my inner knowing and to my soul's purpose here on earth.

The peace I feel after using NuClam is not just mental; it's physical. I feel my cells harmonizing, my mind quieting, and my heart opening. Everything feels aligned, and I am truly at home within myself. Using it daily allows me to tap into my creativity, gratitude, and merriment. It provides a source of energy that always lights me up. At 83, I feel more connected to myself and truly vibrate with a genuine frequency of love, purpose, and enthusiasm for life. I want that for you. I want you, at whatever age you are, to feel the deepest alignment with your essence, that soaring feeling of being perfectly at home within your skin.

If you feel inclined, try NuCalm to welcome you into that sacred space within, where the outside world fades away, and the chatter of the mind grows silent. It's a beautiful reminder that we all have access to this peace if we give ourselves time to unplug and allow healing to happen in our bodies and hearts.

However you navigate the path of self-discovery, healing, and homecoming, I hope you come to understand and accept that everything you need has always been within you. The answers, peace, and sense of belonging are not found in the external world but in the quiet spaces of our hearts. Releasing the need for external validation, you reconnect with your deepest truths and embrace the fullness of the *magic* within you.

The journey home is not about becoming something more but about remembering who we have always been. Whether through moments of stillness or simply tuning into the present moment, we are continually invited to come home to ourselves. This is the *magic*, my friend, to live from a place of wholeness and to trust in the beauty of our unfolding. Homecoming is the greatest gift we get to give ourselves.

"At the center of your being, you have the answer; you know who you are, and you know what you want."

—LAO TZU

Chapter 8

Expectancy Makes it Happen

In the last seven chapters, we've explored powerful tools for awakening the *magic* within you. You've learned how to align with your essence, release what no longer serves you, and nurture the emotions that create a sense of homecoming. Each step has brought you closer to living a life where *magic* feels natural and ever-present.

Now, it's time to unlock the most transformative secret of all: *Expecting Magic.*

Magic isn't something you stumble upon by accident. It begins with a conscious decision to believe that *magic* is real and actively working in your life. This belief shifts your energy and perspective, opening you to see and experience the subtle miracles surrounding you.

When you *Expect Magic*, something extraordinary happens. Anticipation amplifies the flow of energy, aligning your thoughts, emotions, and actions with a frequency that magnetizes and draws *magic* toward you. It seems the Universe listens to your frequency and responds with opportunities, synchronicities, and blessings that seem perfectly timed.

Having such expectations is powerful because it turns passive hope into active participation. Instead of waiting for *magic* to happen, you are looking for it, listening to it, and celebrating it when it arrives. This energy of anticipation creates a magnetic pull, connecting you with the already present *magic* waiting to unfold. When you approach your day with curiosity and excitement, you naturally attune yourself to notice the small wonders and serendipities that others might overlook. A phone call at just the right moment, a conversation that sparks a brilliant idea, or an unexpected opportunity that feels meant to be: these moments aren't random. They are the result of *magic* aligning with your energy and intention.

The more you believe in, expect, and embrace *magic*, the more it will appear in your life. *Magic* responds to your trust and your openness to recognizing it. It isn't something distant or reserved for a select few. It is already here, woven into the fabric of your everyday life, waiting for you to notice and invite it to expand. *Magic* thrives in anticipation. When you expect it, you no longer dismiss synchronicities as mere coincidences. Instead, you see them as gentle reminders that the Universe is working in perfect interrelation with you.

THE POWER OF EXPECTING *MAGIC*

We live in a world that has conditioned us to doubt. From the time we are young, we are taught to seek proof before believing and to wait for something tangible before trusting its presence. We've been led to think that seeing is believing, but *magic* asks us to move beyond these limitations. *Magic* invites us into a higher truth, claiming, 'You already know I am here.'

Think about the moments in your life when you have felt *magic's* undeniable presence. Perhaps it was the perfect synchronicity that led you to a life-changing opportunity or the way your heart swelled with joy at the kindness of a stranger. Maybe it was in the goosebumps you felt when hearing a story that touched your soul or the overwhelming peace that embraced you when you followed an intuitive nudge. These instances are not coincidences. They are gentle yet powerful reminders that *magic* has always been with you.

We don't need more proof. The evidence of *magic* surrounds us—in the beauty of a sunrise, the perfect timing of an unexpected call, the miracle of connection when two souls meet. It is in the stories we hear that lift our spirits, the unexplainable miracles that fill us with wonder, and the inexplicable knowing that sometimes moves through us like a current of divine energy.

Magic isn't something you need to prove or justify. It simply asks you to believe. To trust. To *expect. Magic* responds when you release the need for validation and instead align yourself with its presence. It doesn't hesitate. It flows naturally into your life because it has been waiting for you to recognize it all along.

The world has trained us to be skeptical, to wait for external signs before stepping into belief. But you already hold the most profound proof there is: the moments you have lived, the whispers of truth you've felt, and the knowing that *magic* has already appeared in your life countless times before. Remember a magical experience when you followed an intuitive tap on the shoulder, and it led to a situation that changed your perspective or the way you found just the right words to comfort a friend in need? Think of the times when life felt 'impossibly' aligned, and then you stumbled upon a better job opportunity at the perfect moment or met someone fantastic who became a lifelong friend in the most unexpected happenstance.

Perhaps there have been smaller, quieter instances of *magic,* the way a song came on the radio just when you needed reassurance, or how a child's laughter reminded you of life's simplicity and serendipity. These moments are not random; they are *magic* weaving its way into your life, offering you glimpses of its continual presence.

When you reflect on these experiences, you'll see that *magic* has always existed, waiting patiently for you to recognize it and trust its guidance. Let go of the doubt that has kept you waiting. Move into the space of reverence, where *magic* is no longer something you hope for but something you know is working with and through you. Cultivate it. Expect it. Watch it unfold. When you do, you'll discover that *magic* doesn't just arrive—it shows up!

HOW TO *EXPECT MAGIC* DAILY

To truly invite *magic* into your life, you must embrace an expectant and receptive mindset. This isn't about waiting passively for something extraordinary to happen; it's about actively creating the conditions where *magic* can flourish.

Expectation means shifting your inner dialogue from doubt to possibility. It's waking up each day with a quiet confidence that the Universe is orchestrating moments of alignment and connection just for you. Openness is the willingness to let go of rigid plans and predetermined outcomes, trusting that what unfolds might exceed even your wildest dreams.

When you approach life with this balance of expectation and excitement, you begin to see the extraordinary in the everyday. A new opportunity, a meaningful coincidence, or even an experience of stillness can become a doorway to *magic*. By expecting the best and staying open to how it arrives, you create a partnership with the energy that transforms your life in ways you could never imagine.

Ask yourself, *'What unexpected wonders will today bring?'* This simple shift in perspective changes how you move through the world. You'll begin to notice the subtle ways *magic* weaves into your life. It might appear in a life-defining meeting, a surprise 'yes,' or an emphatic push to take a new direction. The more you expect it, the more it shows up.

Cultivating *magic* into your life is not a one-time action; it is a daily practice, a commitment to devote your time, energy, and intention to expecting the extraordinary. As you nurture a seed by watering it daily, cultivating *magic* requires consistent care and attention. Making *magic* a daily routine means, each morning, choosing to align your heart and mind with the belief that *magic* is already present and actively working for you. This practice goes beyond simply thinking positively. It means anchoring yourself in the certainty that unseen forces are guiding you, even though you cannot yet see the results.

Devotion to expecting *magic* means looking for it in the smallest details of your day and pausing to notice the synchronicities, feeling gratitude for the beauty around you, and staying open to the surprises life has in store. It is found in quiet moments of reflection, trusting your intuition, and stepping forward with unwavering trust.

When you make expecting *magic* a daily practice, it becomes part of the rhythm of your life. Over time, it shifts how you see the world and how the world responds to you, creating a flow of limitless moments filled with magical gifts. *Magic* won't just happen; you have to be at the helm of making it happen and fostering its presence day in and day out.

Here are a few ways to cultivate magic every day:

- **Wake Up with Anticipation**

  Begin each morning with a sense of wonder. Instead of focusing on what you must do, focus on what might unfold. Set the intention to notice and celebrate even the smallest magical moments throughout your day.

- **Trust the Timing**

  Magic has its own pace. When something doesn't go as planned, take a deep breath and trust that it is unfolding perfectly. Often, what feels like a detour is leading you on a more scenic route to where you're meant to be.

- **Respect Every Encounter**

  Approach each person you meet with curiosity and kindness. Every interaction, no matter how brief, holds the potential to shift your perspective or open a new door.

- **Celebrate Small Wins**

  The *magic* of life isn't just in the big moments; it's in the everyday victories. Celebrate the kind words you shared, the goal you worked toward, or the courage you showed. Gratitude for these small happenings amplifies the *magic* around you.

- **Lead with Love and Joy**

  Magic is born in the energy of love and joy. When you approach challenges with compassion and prioritize what brings you happiness, you become a magnet for extraordinary experiences.

Every day is an opportunity to create and expand the *magic* you bring to your life. With every choice, every interaction, and every intention, you contribute to the outcomes you desire. Trust in the *magic* waiting to unfold, and let your actions magnetize the *magic* that wants to appear.

MAGIC HAS ITS OWN SENSE OF TIME.

As we learn to *expect magic*, we grow to anticipate its presence. We move from the expansiveness of *magic* in the quantum field to the expectation of *magic* on our own timeline. Time, as we perceive it, is a human construct. We live by clocks and calendars, marking our days with appointments, deadlines, and schedules. Yet, *magic* doesn't adhere to these constraints. *Magic* does not exist on a clock or follow a schedule. It doesn't concern itself with deadlines, holidays, or the pressure to deliver for a big event. *Magic* operates outside of linear time because it is connected to a higher source—an infinite intelligence that weaves together all things for the highest good of all.

Magic flows from a source that transcends human understanding. This source is infinite, eternal, and deeply connected to the highest good. It operates with an intelligence that takes into account not just your life but the intricate web of all existence. This divine intelligence ensures that *magic* arrives when it is meant to, not when we demand it. Our human need for control, confirmation, or immediate results has no bearing on the timing of *magic*. What matters is our ability to trust, surrender, and align ourselves with its flow.

When we attempt to impose human timing onto *magic,* we diminish its essence. *Magic* is not about catering to the mundane or the frivolous, like securing a parking spot during a busy shopping trip or ensuring perfect weather for an outdoor event. Instead, *magic* is about delivering what is truly needed at precisely the right moment, whether we recognize it at the time or not.

When you *expect magic* to show up in your life, you aren't commanding it to happen on your terms. You are opening your heart to the possibility that the Universe knows exactly when and how to deliver what you need. Trust that *magic* is always working on your behalf, even if it doesn't follow your preferred timeline.

As we explored in Chapter 3, dancing with destiny requires trust, openness, and the willingness to move in rhythm with life's unfolding. *Magic* and destiny are intertwined, working together to guide you toward your highest potential. Destiny is not a fixed, predetermined path. It is a fluid journey shaped by your choices, intentions, and alignment with your essence. *Magic* serves as the unseen partner in this dance, gently nudging you, opening doors, and providing opportunities that align with your soul's purpose.

When you embrace the timeless nature of *magic*, you free yourself from the pressure of immediate results. You sense that delays, detours, and even disappointments can be part of the divine choreography of your destiny. *Magic* is not confined to the urgent needs of the moment. Instead, it works within the grand tapestry of your life, ensuring that everything unfolds in seamless harmony.

Our human desire to control outcomes often creates resistance to the flow of *magic*. We want guarantees, confirmations, and visible signs before we trust that something is appearing. Yet *magic* asks us to let go of this need for control and instead surrender to the infinite intelligence that guides it. Surrender is not about giving up but about releasing your grip on how and when things should happen. It is about trusting that *magic* is always working for your highest good, even if you cannot see the full picture.

To truly invite *magic* into your life, you must shift from a mindset of control to one of partnership. This means trusting that the Universe is co-creating with you, aligning circumstances, people, and opportunities in ways you could never orchestrate alone. This partnership requires faith, patience, and a willingness to relinquish rigid expectations. When you release your need for certainty and instead focus on aligning with your essence, you create the conditions for *magic* to flourish. *Have you ever experienced a time when something didn't go according to plan, only to realize later that it was a blessing in disguise?* Perhaps you missed an opportunity you desperately wanted, only to find a better one waiting for you down the road. These moments are not accidents; they result from *magic* operating on a timeline far more intelligent than our own.

Magic doesn't respond to impatience or doubt; it responds to trust and alignment. The more you focus on raising your frequency, nurturing your essence, and staying true to your path, the more magic will flow into your life. Our attachment to time can limit our ability to experience natural flow. We expect things to happen on our schedule, often overlooking the subtle ways *magic* is already at work. To truly connect with *magic*, we must learn to see beyond the clock and trust in the divine timing of all things. *Magic* operates in the realm of synchronicity, where events align in ways that seem almost too perfect to be true. These moments often happen when we least expect them, reminding us that the Universe has a plan far greater than our own.

For example:
- You might miss a train, only to meet someone on the next one who changes your life.
- You could lose a job only to discover a new path that brings you greater fulfillment.

- A delay in your plans might lead you to the right place at the right time for an opportunity you didn't even know you needed.

These are reminders that *magic* is not concerned with the clock. It is connected to the infinite intelligence of the Universe, which always delivers what is needed at the perfect time. *Magic* is a gift, a sacred connection to the divine flow of life. It is not meant to be wasted on trivial or mundane demands. Instead, treasure this connection and use it to align with your destiny.

When you approach *magic* with reverence, you strengthen your relationship with it. Trust that *magic is* working for your highest good, and let go of the need to use it for immediate or superficial gains. Instead, focus on the bigger picture of your life and the ways *magic* can guide you toward your purpose. Just as you cannot force the rhythm of a dance, you cannot force the timing of *magic*. Instead, stay present, responsive, and open to possibilities that unfold with each step. Trust that *magic* knows the way, and allow yourself to be guided by its grand and giving wisdom.

Magic doesn't conform to the limitations of human schedules or expectations. Instead, it operates in alignment with the infinite intelligence of the Universe, delivering exactly what is needed *when* needed. Your role is not to control *magic* but to trust it. Release the need for proof or confirmation and instead cultivate a sense of faith and alignment. Trust in the journey, and allow it to lead the way magically.

In all the years I have been expecting *magic,* I have learned that *magic* will not come to prove its existence; it arrives when you believe in it and expect it from a place of knowing and interconnectedness. It is by affirming that *magic* is already working for you that *magic* arrives on its timeline. I encourage you to look for the signs that *magic* is and has been in your life. Acknowledge the work it has done, and be enthusiastic about what is yet to come. Whenever I see *magic* unfolding, I celebrate, show my gratitude, and share my thankfulness. The more you are thankful for the *magic* you expect, the more *magic* will dazzle you with its 'presence and presents' in your life. Expecting is an action word, so use it and see what *magic* comes your way.

> *"The world is full of magical things, patiently waiting for our senses to grow sharper."*
>
> —W.B YEATS

Chapter 9

Becoming a
Beacon of *Magic*

There's something profoundly transformative about working on ourselves, not just for our growth but for the ripple effect we create in the world around us. Life, in many ways, mirrors who we are at our core. When we commit to our personal evolution and nurture the *magic* within, it doesn't stay contained. It spreads outwards, touching the lives of those around us in ways we may never fully realize. The unseen yet undeniable *magic* of life is knowing that when we rise, we invite others to do the same.

Our inner world and our actions are deeply interconnected. When we approach a task, a relationship, or a challenge with love, care, and intention, that energy permeates every aspect of our lives. It impacts how we move through the world, treat others, and respond to the circumstances we encounter. Every choice we make, every thought we nurture, every action we take ripples out, leaving an imprint far greater than we know.

As a *beacon of magic*, I invite you to see your life as a beautiful, unfolding conversation. Every action you take, whether big or small, is a precious reflection of your intentions, desires, and energy. Each thought you nurture adds depth to this dialogue, and every decision becomes a message to the world and your soul. Just like a gardener tends to the earth with care, your life is a series of intentional plantings, each contributing to the garden of your legacy. You're not just growing for yourself but creating a lush, vibrant space where others are nourished and inspired by what you've cultivated over time.

Approaching life with this mindset, your every thought becomes an ingredient in the grand recipe of creation. You're constantly incorporating the elements of pleasure, curiosity, and amazement, which create *magic* that touches everything around you. Imagine your actions sending out waves of energy that ripple across the world, touching people, situations, and events in ways you can't even fully comprehend. You engage in a Divine interaction when you choose to show up this way. The energy you put out always returns to you, shaped by your intentions and awareness. It's as if life itself is responding, shaping its answer based on the *magic* you've contributed.

In this divine interplay, you are both the creator and the recipient of the *magic* that flows through your life. Every moment offers a chance to contribute to the conversation, to add to the symphony of experiences and exchanges that make up the resonant harmony of your existence. Whether you realize it or not, every smile, every kind word, every compassionate act sends out vibrations that uplift and inspire those around you.

Think of your life as an ongoing exchange, not just with people but with the entire Universe. The way you choose to think, act, and feel today will shape the experiences of tomorrow. By being mindful of this, you can intentionally craft a life that reflects *the magic* you want to bring into the world and make it delightful. And as you continue to engage in this sacred dialogue, the world listens. It responds, sending back echoes of your light and your love. Your *magic* becomes a part of the collective conversation, a force of positivity that has the power to shift, transform, and elevate. Embrace this role fully, knowing that each moment is a chance to create, communicate, and contribute to the consciousness of *magic* that surrounds us all.

THE RIPPLE EFFECT OF *MAGIC*

When we evolve our beacon of *magic*, the ripple effects are undeniable. Take, for example, someone who begins a daily meditation practice. At first, it may seem like a personal, internal endeavor. Yet, over time, the inner peace they cultivate affects how they show up in their relationships. They become more patient, more compassionate, and more present. Others sense this shift, and without knowing it, they respond differently. The world around them starts to change. This is the *magic* of self-work: what we do within affects the world outside.

Now, suppose you expanded that practice to every area of your life. *What If you approach everything you do intending to be a beacon of magic, a source of light and inspiration for others? How would that change the way you move through the world? How would it impact the way you show up for yourself and the people you love?*

Opening to the outcomes of these questions is the start of a magnificent journey: a journey to self, home, the vastness of the Universe, the infinite realms of the cosmos, and beyond. Each time you unfurl more of the *magic* in your life, you become a beacon of what is possible for you and so many others. The *magic* you cultivate within yourself has a way of expanding far beyond your own life. It reaches into the hearts of others, inspiring them to tap into their own *magic*. And so, the ripple effect grows, spreading light, love, and transformation across the world.

As you reflect on the journey you've taken through these pages, know that your work on yourself is not just for you; it's for everyone you encounter. Each time you show up with intention, choose delight and allow *magic* to materialize, you contribute to the collective *magic*.

You are a part of this greater whole, an essential note in the symphony of existence. As you awaken to this awareness, recognize that with knowledge comes responsibility. Once you understand the *magic* you carry, you cannot return to a place of unknowing. You are now called to nurture and honor this journey, devoted to living with intention and purpose.

As I reflect on the incredible journey my life has taken, I am reminded of how deeply *magic* weaves into every moment. Over the years, I've come to realize that the greatest gift we can offer the world is our light, our unique essence, fully alive. Through my work as a speaker, host, author, and mentor, I've had the immense privilege of helping others step into their power and see themselves as the beacons they truly are.

I've been fortunate enough to touch lives through my books, such as *Send Me Someone: A True Story of Love Here and Hereafter* and *Chicken Soup to Inspire Body and Soul,* guiding countless souls to realize that *magic* isn't something that just happens to us. It's something we cultivate. It's the recognition that we can shape our reality in each moment through our thoughts, intentions, and actions. I've spoken on stages worldwide, led transformative workshops, and mentored individuals ready to step into their next chapter with clarity, grace, courage, and *magic* in their heart.

Yet, beyond the accolades and accomplishments, what fills my spirit most is seeing others rise, watching as they become beacons of *magic* in their own lives. There is a cumulative effect; when we enlighten ourselves, we activate others. We design a world where *magic* is expected and experienced in its fullest, most beautiful form.

I want you to deeply own the fact that *the magic you seek is within you.* You don't have to search for it elsewhere. As someone who has navigated great loss, deep love, and profound change, I can tell you from the depths of my soul that *magic* lives within you as you. Your journey is significant, and the legacy you create—through your actions, words, and presence—leaves an indelible mark on the world.

You don't have to perform grand gestures to become a beacon of *magic.* It's not about doing more but being more intentional with what you already do.

HOW YOU DO ONE THING IS HOW YOU DO EVERYTHING

There's a powerful saying that goes, "How you do one thing is how you do everything." This means the energy you bring to one area of your life inevitably affects all other areas. When you approach life with love, care, and intention, that energy ripples into your relationships, work, health, and overall well-being.

For example, think about how you start your day. If you wake up choosing gratitude and excitement for the possibilities ahead, that energy will carry you through the day. On the other hand, if you open your day feeling rushed, overwhelmed, or anxious, that energy can also color your interactions and experiences. Every step we take in life, every intention we set, leaves an imprint. These imprints aren't fleeting. Each word we speak and each gesture we make create ripples that extend beyond the present moment. The more mindful and intentional we are, the more meaningful and powerful the imprint becomes. We shape the world around us through the imprints we leave behind, each reflecting our innermost selves, influencing the world in ways we may never fully grasp.

This understanding invites us to consider our actions not as isolated events but as seeds planted for the future. These seeds, nurtured by our awareness, blossom into legacies—whether in the hearts of those we touch or the energetic shifts we cause in the collective consciousness. It reminds us to live with the knowledge that our imprints, no matter how small, contribute to the ongoing evolution of our world.

Through this lens, see each moment as a seed you're planting, knowing that every action, word, or thought will blossom into something larger, something far-reaching. Embrace your role as a beacon and trust that the *magic* you cultivate within will radiate outward, touching lives in ways beyond your knowing. Consider yourself a stone dropped into a still pond. Each intention, each act of kindness, creates ripples that extend far beyond what you can see, reaching the farthest edges of your existence. The beauty of life lies in discovering these ripples, in realizing that your light, no matter how small it may seem, has the power to move and inspire others.

We don't always have the answers. The joy is the unfolding journey, the mystery of quantum awareness, and the infinite ways it reveals itself to us. The vastness of all that is mirrors the vastness of your own potential. You are part of something so much greater, an essential thread in the cosmic tapestry, connected to everything and everyone.

Now that you know this truth, there is no turning back. Once awakened, you cannot 'unknow' the power you hold. You have a responsibility to honor this *magic*, to be devoted to the path that beckons you forward, and to live in alignment with the awareness that you are part of a much grander design. Each choice you make is not isolated but woven into the fabric of this collective consciousness, influencing and inspiring those around you.

Knowing something deeply becomes a part of you, shaping your worldview and guiding your actions. True power lies in your ability to act from that knowing. As you move forward, let every step be infused with the *magic* you've cultivated within. You are not just a passenger on this journey but a co-creator, actively shaping the world with your light.

MAGIC TRANSFORMS HUMANITY

Be the ripple, the stone in the pond, the quiet but undeniable force that influences and uplifts everything it touches. Even the smallest act, the quietest moment of presence, has the potential to inspire *magic* in the lives of others. This is your birthright, and by stepping into it fully, you encourage others to do the same.

The truth is that every action we take has the potential to leave an imprint. Every word we speak, gesture we make, and thought we entertain sends ripples outward. The more intentional we are with these actions, the more powerful those ripples become.

Ultimately, the greatest gift we can leave behind is the imprint of who we are, reminiscent of the love we shared, the joy we brought, and the lives we touched. Our legacy using *magic* is not just the accomplishments we achieve or the goals we meet but the energy we infuse into the world. It's the moments when we chose to be kind when it would have been easier to be indifferent. It's the times we chose to show up fully when no one was watching. It's the love we gave without expecting anything in return.

As you become a beacon of *magic* and radiate its transformative power, I invite you to reflect deeply on the legacy of your *magic*. *What kind of imprint will you leave in the hearts of others? How will your unique magic inspire those around you and uplift the world in ways only you can?*

To be a beacon of *magic* is to live with purpose and authenticity. It means standing firmly in who you are and allowing your presence to inspire others to reconnect with their own power. This isn't about striving for perfection. It's about sharing your truth, leading with love, and trusting that every act of compassion, every moment of empathy, and every word of encouragement can spark a ripple of transformation.

Your *magic* doesn't shine in isolation. It thrives in the connections you create and the energy you share with others. Each time you act with love or offer your light freely, you encourage someone else to do the same. This is how *magic* multiplies—through the simple, intentional ways we show up for one another.

Think about the ways you might expand your *magic* into the lives of others. *What gifts can you offer to the people around you, no matter how small they may seem? What truths can you speak that might uplift or inspire?* As you live more fully in your *magic,* you become a living example of what's possible, encouraging others to trust in their own potential and divine connection.

Ask yourself:
- How can I live as a source of inspiration in my everyday interactions?

- Where can I offer more love, even when it feels unexpected or challenging?
- How might my actions create ripples of *magic* that extend far beyond what I can see?

This is not about doing more; it's about being more of who you are. By fully stepping into yourself, you show others how to trust their light. By giving freely of your energy, you invite others to awaken to their own divine possibilities.

The *magic* you share becomes your legacy. It is the love, kindness, and joy you bring to the world that will be remembered. Let your life be a reflection of the *magic* you believe in and the light you wish to see.

Magic Universally

Each day is an opportunity to add to the imprint you're creating. With every choice, every interaction, and every action, you leave behind a trail of *magic* that others can follow. You may not always see your impact, but trust that it's there, quietly unfolding in the lives you universally touch and the souls you indirectly touch. Remember, the *magic* isn't in doing more; it's in being more of who you already are. By living with intention, showing up fully, and sharing your light with the world, you become a beacon of *magic*. Your presence alone has the power to inspire, uplift, and transform.

Going forward, do not just *expect magic*. Become a co-creator of the *magic* that graces the earth. Step fully into your role as a partner with the divine, someone who does not simply wait for *magic* but actively participates in its creation. Be the one who embodies the presence of a beacon, radiating possibility in every interaction you make. It is not only about the big gestures, though they hold significance. It is about the countless small moments that create a ripple effect, touching lives in ways you may never see. An encouraging word, a listening ear, or an act of mercy can expand *magic* in a world that has forgotten *magic* exists.

Let your life be a living example of what is possible when you align with infinite good. Carry the intention of *magic* into everything you do, from how you greet a stranger to how you magnify your dreams. By showing up fully and consistently, you enrich your life and inspire others to believe in and create *magic* exponentially.

Becoming a beacon of *magic* begins with simple, intentional actions that amplify your presence and energy.

1. **Practice Presence:** One of the simplest yet most profound ways to become a beacon of *magic* is by being fully present with others. In a world filled with distractions, your presence is a gift. When fully engaged in conversation, when you listen deeply, when you show up with undivided attention, you create a space where *magic* can unfold. People feel seen, heard, and valued, creating a ripple effect of positivity.

2. **Celebrate Small Wins:** So often, we wait for big achievements to celebrate, but the *magic* of life is found in the small, everyday victories. Acknowledge your progress, no matter how tiny it seems. *Did you show kindness to a stranger? Did you take a step toward a long-term goal?* Celebrate these moments. As you honor the little wins, you cultivate a gratitude mindset, which becomes contagious.

3. **Lead with Love:** Whether you're interacting with a loved one, a colleague, or a stranger, lead with love. Love is the highest vibration we offer, and it has the power to transform everything it touches. You shift the energy when you choose to approach situations from a place of inclusion rather than fear or judgment. You become a vessel through which the *magic* of love flows, creating more harmony and connection in your relationships.

4. **Nurture Joy:** Being a beacon of *magic* isn't just about spreading light to others and nurturing joy within yourself. Take time to do the things that make you feel alive and engaged as your inner child. Play, dance, laugh, create. When you tap into your own joy, you automatically lift the energy of those around you. Joy is magnetic, and it draws much more *magic* into your life.

These practices not only enrich your life but also create a reverberation of positivity, inspiring *magic* in the world around you.

MAGIC IS FOREVER

Magic is not fleeting. It is eternal, ever-present, and boundless. It weaves itself into the moments of our lives, often unnoticed, yet always ready to shine when we open our hearts to it. *Magic* is the thread that connects us to one another and to the infinite possibilities of the Universe.

Throughout these pages, we have explored how to awaken and nurture this *magic*, to see it not as a rare occurrence but as a constant presence. *Magic* is forever because it exists in all of us, an infinite source of light and love waiting to be shared. It is not confined to a single moment, a specific achievement, or even one lifetime. It transcends time, carrying its brilliance through every connection we make and every cascade we create.

Together, we form a radiant constellation of *magic*, each of us shining uniquely. This isn't just about individual light but the collective glow we create when we come together. Your *magic* matters. It adds to the brilliance of the whole, lighting the way for others to see their own power and possibility.

My deepest hope is that, as you've read through these pages, you've felt a profound sense of belonging and an invitation to continue your journey of discovering the *magic* you've always carried within. You are here for a reason, a unique purpose that echoes in the stars above and resonates in the very fabric of this Universe. Never doubt the quiet yet immense power you hold to change lives simply by being your authentic self.

I invite you to marvel at this ongoing dance with life. Embrace the *magic* within you and move boldly into the world as a beacon of love, light, and transformation. Let your actions, presence, and essence vibrate outward, creating surges of inspiration. Remember, the most profound *magic* is not something outside of you—it is the infinite *magic* that lives in you.

As you carry the *magic* you've discovered into the world, hold close to this truth: *you are the sparkle in someone's day, the twinkle in the infinite sky, and the wonder the Universe has been waiting for. So dance freely in the brilliance of your light. Sprinkle your magic generously, touch lives wherever you go, and trust that the best is still to come.*

Shine brightly, beautiful soul. The world is waiting for your magic, and I, too, cannot wait to see the miraculous imprint you will create.

> *"Magic is believing in yourself; if you can do that,*
> *you can make anything happen."*
>
> — JOHANN WOLFGANG VON GOETHE

Chapter 10

Wait...Encore!

In a theater, an *Encore* is a request for more! It is a recognition that what has just unfolded is so impactful that it deserves to continue. Life, in many ways, offers us the same opportunity. Just when we think a chapter is closing, life calls us back, asking us to dig deeper, share more of our authentic selves, and live with a renewed sense of purpose.

Imagine the artist who, after completing a masterpiece, is asked to create again, not because the original wasn't enough, but because what was shared has sparked something greater. Just as a painter or musician returns to the canvas or stage, life's Encore Moments invite us to step forward *once more*, bringing our deepened wisdom and creativity to a new, unfolding expression.

Encores are a call to contribute more of who we are in ways we may not yet have discovered, offering our light and gifts to the world. The word "Encore" beckons us to bring forth what remains unseen, to share the gifts still inside us. It's not a return to the past, nor a repeat of what's already been performed. Instead, an Encore in life is a chance to deepen our essence, embody all we have become, and offer the world our truest gifts.

I love the word "Encore" because it holds such personal meaning. For me, it's a word that whispers, *"There's more to give, more beauty to share."* Encore invites me to lean in and offer what's most true, the as-yet unexpressed parts of myself that have been shaped by everything I've lived through. It's not about going back, nor is it about redoing anything. Instead, an Encore is a return to the stage of life with everything I am right now. It is a culmination of experiences, love, and wisdom I didn't have before.

To desire an encore is to feel a prompt that *there's still magic to create, still gifts you have yet to reveal.* And so, I've learned to treat each new life passage as an invitation to offer myself in a new way. In these times, I create from a fresh place of love and intention and show the world all of me unfiltered, evolved, and whole in my being.

Consider how a tree returns each season, pouring its energy into a new bloom, regardless of how many seasons have passed. It doesn't stop creating beauty or bearing fruit simply because it's grown tall or weathered. Each spring, the tree embraces an Encore, reaching for more sunlight, stretching its roots deeper into the earth, and giving back to the world in full color once more. In this way, we, too, are invited to grow beyond what we've known, to share ourselves fully, and to create new levels of beauty and meaning with the turning of every new season of our lives.

I believe an Encore is a reminder that each of us can offer something beautiful to the world, something uniquely ours, no matter our age, accomplishments, or setbacks. As long as we have breath, we have the opportunity to step forward and bestow our presence over and over again in a manner that makes an Encore a precious gift for everyone.

At my age, an Encore is far more than a precious gift; it is the permission to move beyond what I have always done and exuberantly refine my gifts and all I may offer. After decades of working, producing, and entertaining, I now live to elevate. I wake up each morning with an irrepressible, bubbling exuberance because I am drawn to love what I see, appreciate what I have, and give openly and imaginatively. Having followed all the steps I have shared in this book, the Divine continually bestows bountiful *magic* in friendships, connections, laughter, and creativity. I have moved beyond any constructs to bask in the presence of something so much bigger than me: a higher intelligence, a more enlightened consciousness. I'll admit it has taken many years to get here, but they have been spectacular years, laced with the wonder and beauty of every magical moment one could ask for.

THE BEAUTY OF THE ENCORE

The beauty of an Encore is that it doesn't ask us to reinvent ourselves but to showcase our essence. We get to bring forward the wisdom, love, and joy we've gathered, offering us room to grow in new directions. We're not called to start over but to continue expanding our unique nature, refining our talents, and amplifying our capacity to live fully and uninhibited.

Living in an Encore is both an invitation and a challenge to immerse our hearts in *all* that we do. It calls us to embrace the power of the 'next act' that draws on everything we've learned, loved, and lived, layering it with newfound wisdom. In this light, Encore becomes our chance to take the stage repeatedly with a deeper clarity, a lighter heart, and a more playful spirit.

As we embody the vibrancy of Encore, life ceases to be about reaching a final destination and becomes a beautiful dance of stepping onto the stage with anticipation. We do so with more heart, humor, and emergent energy each time. Encore is a desire to live boldly, to bring forward the best of ourselves, and to relish the *magic* in the journey as we go.

As a practice, living an Encore might mean reconnecting with the qualities you cherish most about yourself. Perhaps you decide to finally pursue that adventure you've always dreamed about or open up about a passion you've hidden away. Maybe you dive back into your art or music with more intensity, less perfectionism, and a greater fondness for the process itself. Each time you choose to revisit what makes you come alive, you're giving the world a part of you it will truly adore.

Imagine your Encore as an invitation to live with fearless generosity: sharing your wisdom with others, taking risks that deepen your purpose, and leaning into what delights you continuously. With every bold choice and joyful act, you make the Encore a divine part of your life. In this way, *Encore* isn't just a desire to *do* something great; it's the magical unfolding of who you are becoming in the next iteration of you. Stepping onto the stage of life, time and time again, ready to offer more depth, love, and joy, we celebrate life's journey.

Take a moment right now to pause and think about the times when life invited you to show up and perform an Encore. These moments are often filled with emotions, excitement, curiosity, and sometimes even nervousness and hesitancy. Too often, as we move through different stages of life, we believe that our greatest contributions are behind us. Yet, every experience and challenge has prepared us for a brand new Encore. Let's accept the invitation to bring forward what is most meaningful, to embrace the wisdom we've gained, and to share ourselves in ways we may have never considered.

AN INVITATION TO REFLECT

I recently attended a beautiful Celebration of Life ceremony where I witnessed firsthand the true beauty of someone living in an Encore manner. Family and friends shared stories and memories, each revealing facets of this person's life that exemplified the essence of showing up repeatedly each time. Many of us had the joy to witness his devotion to giving all of himself in every way he knew. His life, celebrated in that soulful gathering, became a tapestry woven together from countless acts of kindness, resilience, and deeply genuine accomplishments. He was an artist, a creator, and a friend to many, yet he lived with humility and grace, rarely discussing all he had achieved. That ceremony, showcasing his many Encores, revealed how powerful it is to celebrate life as a culmination of everything we have become.

In honoring him, I realized how each of us carries a legacy as intricate and beautiful as a tapestry woven from the threads of our lives. Experiences, connections, and acts of kindness we've conveyed have become part of our unique tapestry, even if we aren't always conscious of it. *What if, instead of waiting for that final bow, we celebrate and honor our legacy, drawing forth the tenderness within us for all to see?*

If we could deeply witness our own legacy, it would give us a profound opportunity to reflect: *What aspects of our lives would we want to see celebrated most vividly? What relationships, achievements, and gestures of kindness would we wish to be remembered? Would we be satisfied with the mark we left, or would there be parts of ourselves we hadn't fully allowed to shine?* Life, after all, is brief. If given the chance to live with renewed intent, what dreams would we be eager to bring to life? Would we choose to be more loving, more honest, or more devoted?

Through the lens of an Encore, we can see that our lives, in all their complexity and beauty, are worthy of recognition at every stage, not just at the end. We can view the multiple facets of our lives and choose to live our Encore with intentionality and heart. This is a choice we may make with full awareness to bring forth our hidden gifts and share more deeply with those around us. In doing so, we create our own standing ovation, a personal recognition of a life worthy of being celebrated continuously.

Imagine, for a moment, being a guest at your celebration of life. Picture the people gathered, their voices soft with remembrance, laughter mingling with tears as they recount stories and small, tender moments woven with grand adventures that together create a portrait of how you lived. *What stories would you wish to hear? What memories, relationships, and contributions would you hope left an enduring impact on those you touched?*

On reflection, you might realize that the qualities others admire most in you are those you may not have fully appreciated or nurtured in yourself. Maybe you've seen these traits in others yet never gave your-self the same gift. You might also notice that people don't dwell on the unfinished projects or dreams left behind. Instead, they celebrate your essence, not the things you didn't accomplish. Such reflection might just be the spark you need to take more chances, follow your passions with greater intention, and be fully present with those you love. Most importantly, it may serve as a reminder to live each day purposefully, knowing that every moment contributes to a life of rich meaning, depth, and significance.

I've learned our lives are not just a collection of memories but an ongoing, intentional creation, an Encore, of everything we hold most dear. In every aspect of life, our actions are our true legacy, and the threads we weave today will one day be the stories others remember, the wisdom they carry forward, and the love that continues to ripple outward.

When we live with this perspective, on the brink of each Encore, we newly imagine the life we will have. Instead of waiting for a time when we're 'ready' or 'pausing' on our dreams, we'll encourage ourselves to *be* that joyous gift to others. We'll allow ourselves to embody our magnificence fully and enthusiastically step into each unique Encore with internal glee. When we do so, *magic* truly unveils itself, revealing more, offering guidance, and showing us exactly who we were destined to be.

YOUR LIFE AS A WORK OF ART

As we reflect on our lives through the lens of *Encore*, we begin to see how every moment, decision, and interaction has become an opportunity to create something meaningful. This is when we realize that each experience, relationship, and choice we make becomes a brushstroke on the canvas of who we are. The dark and light moments, the successes and the hardships, all create the contrast that gives life its complexity. This is *chiaroscuro* at its best. The interplay of light and dark adds richness and depth to our legacy.

Our lives are a dance of joy and sorrow, love and loss, hope and challenge. And it's the people we touch, who stand with us and encourage us, who spark our desire to make each moment count.

Visualize yourself standing center stage, observing the audience filled with the people who have shaped your life and who have loved, supported, and cheered you on. These are the people who have witnessed your journey, who have seen you at your best *and* your worst. They are not there to judge but to applaud the fullness of who you are. They leap to their feet as the curtain opens. A standing ovation before you even begin.

Now, envision saying to each of them: "Thank you for being a part of my journey. Thank you for *your* tender gifts. Here is what I have to give next, and I give it with all my heart." This is when you step into mastering your life, grateful for your gifts and those who shared them with you. This is the essence of an Encore—a *living* celebration of life, a tribute to everything you have become, and a commitment to everything you have yet to offer.

Too often, we relinquish the power we have over our own lives. We acquiesce, give in, and succumb to the mundane, the dull, and the *lifeless*. It is precisely in these moments that we must grab hold of what we hold dear and be the witness to our own greatness, as if we were in that audience, looking upon ourselves, cheering with all our might. At the height of the Encore, you must be your own devoted fan and biggest cheerleader. You must wield the wand that will determine where you end up. No one can do this for you, so you must become the one curating your experiences and deciding what is next. For some, this may involve creating something tangible, like a new career, relationships, or a project that celebrates more of life. For others, it might mean something more heartfelt, like passing down wisdom, values, or traditions to those you care about. Whatever form your Encore takes, it must be with a sense of honoring oneself while also giving back with excitement and relevance.

In many ways, an Encore is a declaration. It is a welcoming of the *magic* yet to come. It is also an acknowledgment that we are still here, still growing, still capable of basking in the delight of our evolution. One of my favorite memories from childhood is of sitting in the backseat of my father's car, telling him, "I can't wait." Somewhat puzzled, he said, "That's silly. Obviously, you *can* wait." Despite his scrutiny, that childlike wonder, the excitement for what's next, is the spirit of Encore. The energy keeps us looking forward, wanting more, eager for the *magic* yet to be revealed.

Embracing the Encore spirit, we can explore and follow paths that call to us. Gone is the weight of past responsibilities so that we may move forward with only the most essential, beautiful parts of ourselves. This freedom, this lightness, allows us to welcome each day as a new performance and opportunity to share the gifts we have cultivated. The Encores of our lives are about embracing what truly matters, allowing us to lean into the finest parts of ourselves, offer our greatest gifts to the world, and inspire others with the *magic* within them.

LIVING AN ENCORE LIFE

An encore is not a repetition; it's the next, more profound iteration of ourselves. It is a moment in life when we step into a new phase with the delight and wonder of a child who 'can't wait' for what's next. In this phase, we welcome the unknown with open arms, full of curiosity, excitement, and a sense of adventure. Just as a child eagerly anticipates the next thrilling moment, living an Encore life calls us to enthusiastically embrace our next chapter.

Less than a year ago, I stood at the threshold of yet another reinvention, my heart both trembling and singing with the audacity of it all. They say wisdom comes with age, but perhaps the truest wisdom lies in knowing when to let go and embrace the unknown with the same wonder that carried us through our younger years.

My Palm Springs condo, once a sanctuary of comfortable certainty for me and my late husband Ted, felt more and more like a beautiful cage of accumulated possessions. The decision to sell it wasn't just about changing addresses—it was about choosing freedom over familiarity, possibility over predictability. As I prepared to shed 90% of my belongings, I learned that each item I touched tells a story, but not all stories need to be carried forward.

Inspired by the Dalai Lama's practice of giving ceremonial scarves, I've found profound joy in transforming my collection of exquisite scarves into bridges of connection. Each scarf, carefully chosen for someone who has touched my spirit, becomes more than fabric—it becomes a tangible expression of gratitude, a way of saying "I see the light in you" without words.

In its infinite wisdom, the Universe had an even grander plan than my modest dreams of a small guest house or casita. Life's promise revealed itself when my daughter Lexi, navigating her own transition through divorce and an empty nest, joined her story with mine. Together, we discovered a home that transcends mere shelter—a gracious space that holds both our separate journeys and our shared path forward.

This 'encore performance' of life required a special kind of courage, the courage to trust that letting go creates space for unexpected magnificence. The process of shedding possessions became a meditation on what truly matters: not the things we own but the connections we nurture, the beauty we share, and the light we bring to each other's lives.

I'm learning once again that voluntary simplicity isn't about deprivation but liberation. Each item I choose to keep must earn its place by being either meaningful or beautiful, preferably both. In this careful curation of my life's physical manifestation, I find myself becoming lighter, freer, and more attuned to essentials.

The *magic* of this transformation lies not just in its outcome—though the shared home with Lexi exceeded all my hopes—but in the journey itself. Becoming a 'joyful gypsy' at eighty-plus isn't about wandering; it's about moving purposefully toward authenticity, toward simplicity, toward the kind of legacy that can't be stored in boxes or displayed on shelves.

This encore, this beautiful reset, reminds me that it's never too late to begin again. That courage, when braided with trust and seasoned with wisdom, can lead us to places more wonderful than we dared imagine. Ultimately, the most precious possession I've kept is the ability to say 'yes' to life's continuing adventure, to embrace change not as my enemy but as my dance partner in this magnificent finale.

Decide that your Encore is a reawakening of your life's most fulfilling moments while stepping forward with renewed energy. Envision diving into relationships, interests, and dreams with a zest that turns ordinary experiences into powerful expressions of who you truly are. Be all about asking, "What more is possible?" and stepping forward; the best is yet to come.

If you want to magnify your Encore and make it a bold declaration to the universe, here are some suggestions for grand, magnificent expressions of your Encore spirit, saying yes to even more.

Magnifying Your Encore: Grand and Monumental Gestures

- **A Pilgrimage:** *What if you took a spiritual or personal journey to a place you've always felt drawn to?* Perhaps it's a sacred site, a historical landmark, or even the hometown of a personal hero. The journey might become an expression of renewal, seeking, and arriving at a deeper understanding of yourself.
- **Creating a Legacy Project:** *What if you start something that will live on beyond you, like a scholarship fund, a community program, or a creative body of work that reflects your passions and values?* This can be as simple as writing a memoir

or crafting an illuminated journal that tells stories of your personal journey and the lessons you've learned.

- **Hosting a Life Celebration:** *What could show up if you organize an event, not as a goodbye but as a joyful celebration of life?* Invite friends, family, and loved ones to share stories, music, and laughter. It's not about closing a chapter but celebrating the beauty of the present and the potential of what's still to come.

- **Daring to Reinvent:** Imagine making a bold career change, relocating to a place you've always dreamed of, or pursuing a dream that may seem improbable but excites you nonetheless. Reinventing yourself with courage and faith can create the ultimate encore—one that showcases your ability to evolve and thrive in any phase of life.

By expanding into your Encore, you declare to the world that you are not done; you're once more getting started. Whether through small actions or grand gestures, you're stepping forward, ready for what comes next with enthusiasm, grace, and openness to possibility.

Although an Encore can feel big, even monumental, you can begin doing some mini Encores immediately. Here are a few examples of how you can cultivate a new Encore in your life easily. These are the main areas where an Encore moment can feel effortless and deeply rewarding. These are the everyday Encores you can cultivate repeatedly.

Magnifying Your Encore: Easy and Continuous Gestures

· **An Encore of Connection:** Reaching out to old friends, calling up family members, or organizing a gathering that celebrates the bonds you've built over a lifetime. You might revive a tradition, like hosting a seasonal dinner, where everyone shares a story or a dream. Each connection brings your presence fully alive in those relationships.

· **An Encore of Adventure:** Taking on the adventure you've always dreamed about but never pursued. Like a hiking expedition, a solo travel experience, or even skydiving. It's about immersing yourself in something that excites you and reminds you that boldness doesn't fade with time; it grows richer and more empowering.

· **An Encore of Creativity:** Picking up an art form that once brought you joy, whether it's painting, dancing, or writing. Imagine returning to your craft without the pressure for perfection, simply creating for the love of it, finding beauty in the process itself. Each brushstroke, dance step, or word becomes a celebration of self-expression and joy.

· **An Encore of Giving:** Volunteering, mentoring, or even starting a new community initiative. Whether it's offering your skills to others, teaching a class, or becoming a mentor, your generosity becomes a legacy of encouragement and guidance, creating ripples that reach far beyond the moment.

I encourage you to bring the spirit of Encore into your everyday life. Try reconnecting with an old friend to reminisce and laugh about your favorite adventures together but this time, with even more appreciation for the time shared. *Or what about reigniting a passion for art or writing that you had set aside, approaching it not as something to be perfected but as an invitation to express and create with newfound freedom?* Perhaps your encore is mentoring others with lessons and skills you've learned, knowing your experiences can spark their dreams of success.

I love Encore moments at home: gathering family around the table, sharing a meal, and fresh stories and memories that give it meaning. In this way, each dinner becomes a call for more connection, intimacy, and appreciation, making moments richer with each gathering.

Encore can also be a call to revisit an old dream, to ask yourself, "What would make my heart sing again?" Maybe it's traveling to a place that once filled you with wonder, picking up an instrument, or dusting off a journal. These aren't 'do-overs'; they're re-imaginings woven with wisdom and perspective you bring to them now. Each time you choose to revisit what makes you come alive, you're giving the world an Encore of your exquisite essence.

CELEBRATING LIFE'S DEFINING MOMENTS

If you're having difficulty defining your next Encore or wondering if you've already lived it, a simple exercise can help you gain clarity and see the greater meaning behind the path you've already traveled to date.

Life's defining moments often offer insights into the direction we're meant to take. Reflecting on them can guide us toward our next evolution and help us see the Encore we might feel drawn to expand next.

One way to bring these moments into focus is to make a list of the three most pivotal years in your life. These are the years when everything changed, your perspective shifted, and you began seeing life through a new lens. For me, one of those years was when we lost everything. Financial hardship decimated our lives, and my future seemed bleak. Another was the year Paul was diagnosed with terminal cancer and the decisions that *had* to be made. The third was when I met Ted, who would become my future husband just two months after Paul's passing. So much transition engulfed me. These were not easy times, but they demanded shifts that reshaped my understanding of life, teaching me how light and dark work together to create the fullness of our existence.

When reflecting on your pivotal years, ask yourself: *What did I learn? How did I grow? What strengths did I discover within myself?* These passages are not simply memories; they are gifts. Each is a piece of the larger story that makes up your life. The lessons you find within these times can offer a blueprint for your next Encore, guiding you in what you want to bring forward into this next phase of your existence.

If you're unsure about your next steps, start with a look back. Your Encore is often hidden in the experiences you've already lived, waiting to be brought into the light. *What actions have you taken that truly brought you alive?* By honoring your history, you honor yourself, and in doing so, you find yourself writing the next chapter of your journey with intention and purpose.

What a journey writing this book has been. What a vital part of this next Encore, a personal journey of reflection, healing, and creation. Over the past few years, I've been confronted with moments that could have easily made me want to retreat. I faced losses that took my breath away, challenges that tested my strength, and setbacks that seemed insurmountable. Yet, instead of letting them define me, I asked myself, *How can I turn all of this into something positive? How can I take the pain, the growth, and the wisdom that life has gifted me and offer it back to the world as something meaningful?* This book became the answer to that question.

Pouring my insights, heart, and stories into these pages has been a beautiful and powerful way for me to create an Encore. It has been an opportunity to revisit the most profound moments of my life, not just for my own understanding but to offer you the lessons and *magic* that have unfolded along the way. Writing this book has been about reliving the past and transforming it into a new offering, a gift I hope will inspire you as you embark on your own Encore.

In many ways, the creation of this book has felt like divine orchestration. There was a flow to it, a sense of ease that could only come from being aligned with something greater than myself. I wasn't just writing; it felt as though I was listening as if these words were already floating in the ether, waiting to be brought to life. Through every chapter, I found myself both reflecting on my past and imagining the future, weaving together the threads of my experiences into something that could serve. I felt the undeniable presence of *magic* guiding the process, reminding me that no matter where we find ourselves in life, there is always more for us to do, more love to share, and more beneficence to give.

This work, this *Encore*, has been a testament to the idea that life is never about stopping or settling. It's about taking everything that has come before– the joys, heartbreaks, and lessons– and turning them into something fresh, something powerful. It has been about realizing that no matter our age or how many chapters we've written, another chapter is always waiting to unfold. And it's up to us to decide what that chapter will reveal.

I know that for many of us elders, there are moments when we wonder if our best days are behind us, if we've already given all we have to give. But I can promise you this: there is always more. There is always another Encore waiting to step into, another gift waiting to be shared. You are not finished yet. You are still growing, still capable of creating *magic* in your life and the lives of others.

For me, this book has been a powerful reminder of the possibilities that still lie ahead. It has reignited my passion for living, creating, and offering my gifts to the world. It has reminded me that each day is a preview for the next and that every moment is a stepping stone toward something greater. We are all called to live our lives with intention, passion, and a deep sense of purpose, knowing that each day is not just the end of a journey but the beginning of another Encore.

As I sit here, reflecting on what this journey has meant, I feel deeply grateful for the opportunity to share it with you. I hope these pages have touched your heart, inspired you to see the *magic* in your life, and given you the courage to step into your own Encore. We all have something more to share with the world. No matter what has come before, the future is full of possibilities, and we only have to reach out and claim them. I know, without a doubt, that you can create something beautiful and meaningful, leaving an enduring legacy in your life while being a beacon of light for someone else.

This book is my Encore. *What will yours be?*

Take a moment to let that question settle into your heart. *What do you feel stirring inside? What desires, dreams, and untapped potential are quietly waiting for you to notice?* The beauty of an Encore is that it isn't confined to a stage or a specific time in life. It's the moment when you decide to step forward again, to reawaken the parts of yourself that may have been dormant or overlooked. It's your invitation to revisit what lights you up and offer it to the world in a new, more profound way.

Your Encore doesn't have to be grand or public; it simply needs to be true. It can be a personal commitment or diving headfirst into something new. Whatever form it takes, your Encore is the gift you give to yourself first, and by living fully, you are a shining mirror.

Think back to all the versions of you that have existed so far: the child full of wonder, the dreamer with boundless hopes, the adult who's weathered storms and celebrated victories. Each of those versions of you has something to offer, something to carry forward into your next chapter. An Encore is never about beginning again; it's about embracing the finest parts of who you are, the lessons you've learned, and the love you've given, allowing them to guide you into the next, more radiant blossoming of your journey. It's not about getting it perfect. It's about showing up with your heart wide open. It's about stepping into each day with the same eagerness and curiosity you felt as a child when you couldn't wait for the next fun thing.

In saying 'yes' to this book and having read this far, I encourage you to say YES! to your next Encore. Allow yourself to discover what's within you and be unapologetic about it. Step into your most authentic expression with a deep and unwavering trust that who you are and all you have become is more than enough. Fully embrace your next Encore, acting without hesitation, knowing life still holds so much more for you to experience, create, and share. If you say yes, *how might that enhance the way you move through your days? How would it impact how you show up for yourself, others, and the world around you?*

This level of willingness allows *magic* to multiply. It produces more ease, joy, and drive, supporting a momentous new journey still waiting to unfold. This is the *magic* of living an Encore life: the understanding that each of us is here for a reason, and that reason is meant to expand during every season of life. In fact, you are a work of *magic* in progress, never finished, always enhancing. Your Encore is that invitation to be both the artist and the masterpiece.

I invite you to ask yourself: *What will my Encore be? What parts of my soul have I been waiting to express? What dreams have I set aside, and how can I bring them to life with more depth and clarity? How can I give myself permission to live boldly and embrace life's richness with open arms? What aspect of me is the world just waiting to see?*

As you ponder these questions, know the answers are alive within you, waiting for your inquiry. Your Encore is your unique expression of everything you've experienced, learned, and been involved in. And as you step into this next chapter, trust that the universe is cheering you on, just as those in your audience have been doing all along.

Living an *Encore* life becomes a call to celebrate each moment, delve into happiness, and offer our best selves to the world around us. Let this be the start of your *Encore* and your definitive call to welcome the journey. Say "Yes, please, Universe" to all who are possible to you.

This is your time.

This is your moment.

Let your Encore be a celebration of everything you are and everything you are yet to become.

Your life is now a magical one person show
The stage is yours.

The next question is…*what will you do with it?*

How will you expect magic and live your Encore?

> *"Life isn't about finding yourself. It's about creating yourself."*
> — George Bernard Shaw

Chapter 11

The *Magic* of YOU!

"The best way to predict your future is to create it."

—Abraham Lincoln

As we reach this book's final pages, I want to reflect on every-thing we've explored together. This journey has been one of discovery, reflection, and, above all, *magic*. From the very first chap-ter, I set out to remind you of something powerful: life is filled with *magic*, and you, my dear reader, are a beacon of that *magic*. It is within you. It always has been. The time has come for you to fully embrace it.

Throughout these chapters, we've discussed the many ways to invite *magic* into your life. We've explored the importance of curiosity, asking *what if* questions, and allowing wonder to guide your path. We've delved into the mystery and beauty of the quantum field, where science and spirituality meet and where anything is possible. We've opened the door to infinite potential, reminding you that your life is a masterpiece waiting to be painted, a symphony waiting to be played.

As I write these words, I want you to feel the deep love and connection I feel for you. My intention has always been to remind you that *magic* is not something reserved for a select few; it's something you get to access every day. It's in the air you breathe, the connections you make, the dreams you dare to follow. *Magic* is in the subtle moments, the quiet whispers of intuition, the flashes of inspiration that guide you forward.

Reflecting on everything we've explored together, I'm filled with a deep sense of gratitude. Gratitude to you, dear reader, for walking this journey with me, for trusting me with your time, and for allowing me to share my heart and experiences with you. This book, this exploration of *magic* and life, has been a way for me to offer all that I've learned in my years of love, loss, adventure, and transformation. Yet, it has also been the beginning of an Encore journey for you and me.

I hope that the pieces I have shared will *ignite* something within you, something magical, something that stirs your soul and enlivens your heart. Something that will inspire you to step boldly into your future and transcend anything that may have been holding you back. Life will always present challenges, but it will also present opportunities, and I want to encourage you to walk into those spaces with an open heart, trusting that there's always more for you to experience and create. And that the *magic* we seek is not out there, in the distance, but inside us, woven into our very being, waiting to be brought to light.

Although this book is coming to a close, your journey is far from over. In fact, it's just beginning. The *magic* we've explored together is yours to carry forward into every corner of your life. From this moment on, I encourage you to *expect magic daily*. Expect it in the little things—the morning sun, the sound of laughter, the kindness of a stranger. Expect it in the big things—the dreams you've yet to live, the synchronicities on their way to you, the transformations burgeoning to unfold.

You are the artist of your life. You have the brush in your hand, and every day, every decision, and every small act of courage adds a new stroke to the canvas of your existence. Life is your work of art, an infinite masterpiece, and you are the one fashioning your future. You are the one with the power to envision how your *magic* unfolds.

This book may be finished, but your work is far from over, and I would love nothing more than to continue this journey with you. I want to invite you to stay connected with me. Whether you seek guidance, mentorship, or just a space to nurture your soul, I'm here. I believe in the *magic* of connection, in the alchemy that happens when two hearts come together with a shared purpose.

If you want to deepen this connection, I invite you to join me for *Tea with Diana*, my personal newsletter, where I share thoughts, reflections, and stories from my heart to yours. It's a sacred space where we can continue to explore the *magic* of life together, where I offer musings, inspiration, and practical guidance for living with purpose and joy. It's like sitting down for tea, just you and me, sharing the wonders of designing a beautiful life.

If you're ready to start your own Divine Dialogue or learn more about journaling as a tool for transformation, visit my website, www.DianaWentworth.com, where I share resources to help you connect with your inner wisdom and create a life filled with *magic* and grace.

I also offer one-on-one coaching and mentoring for those who feel called to dive even deeper. This is my way of walking alongside you, helping you uncover the gifts within, and supporting you as you step into your own *magic*. Nothing is more rewarding than seeing someone light up as they realize how powerful and capable they are. My mission is to help you create the life you desire, one filled with meaning, purpose, and boundless promise. Together, we will chart the course toward your most authentic and joyful self.

Perhaps you're ready to explore new paths, take bold risks, or simply need a gentle nudge to trust your intuition. I'd love to help you navigate those waters to guide you in living your best life with all the heart and soul you were meant to share with the world.

Magic isn't something that happens to you; it's something you create. It's the energy you bring to every experience, the love you infuse into every moment, the joy you allow yourself to feel. You are the *magic.* And as you move forward, I want you to remember that the Universe is always conspiring in your favor, always ready to meet you where you are and offer you more than you ever thought possible.

In every moment, with every choice, you have the power to create something beautiful. The *magic* that lives within you is not something to be hidden away. It is something to be shared, something to be celebrated, something that the world needs. Envision yourself as a lighthouse, standing tall and strong, your light shining out into the world. This light is your *magic,* wisdom, love, and all your unique gifts. As you shine, you become a beacon for others, guiding them, inspiring them, and reminding them of their own inner light. This is how *magic* illuminates. When you live in this way, you give others permission to do the same.

That means there's also more to come from me. Writing this book has been such a profound experience, and I know that my next creative chapters are already stirring within me. This book has been my

Encore, but there are more stories to tell, more wisdom to share, and more ways to offer my love and encouragement. My next books are already waiting to come to life, and I hope you'll join me for them. We're just getting started. The *magic* will continue and will live on.

I want you to take a moment right now to reflect on the journey we've taken together. Think about the lessons you've learned, the insights you've gained, and the ways in which your perspective about *magic* has shifted. *Can you feel magic pulsing within you? Can you sense delight and possibilities waiting for you as a new promise for your future?* This is your time to step into your *magic* fully, without hesitation, without doubt. You are ready for this.

As I wrap up this final sharing, I want to leave you with one last reminder: *always Expect Magic.* Wherever you go, in whatever you do, expect that *magic* to be at play in your life. Trust that the universe is conspiring in your favor and that each moment holds the potential for wonder and transformation. When you *Expect Magic,* you invite it in. You create space for miracles, and you open your entire being to possibilities that await.

Whether stepping into a new chapter, exploring a new passion, or simply savoring the beauty of the present, know that the *magic* is there. It is your birthright. It is your divine assignment. *Magic* has always been there and will continue to show up for you as long as you keep showing up for yourself.

Thank you, from the bottom of my heart, for allowing me to be a part of your journey. I hope this book awakened your soul and reminded you of the beauty of a *magic*-filled life. I'll be here, cheering you on, celebrating your wins, and supporting you with admiration and joy.

The key is always to *Expect Magic* and always believe. I know, without a doubt, that whatever you do, it will be beautiful, meaningful, and uniquely all you.

Until we meet again, remember to *Expect Magic,* and *magic* will be with you.

With love, fierce devotion, and gratitude,

Diana

Thank you

To my beloved late husband, Paul von Welanetz, whose vision conjured flourishing communities. Your soul dances in every gathering, and your depth of partnership over twenty-five years still whispers the comfort of our shared love into my quiet moments.

To the wizards and wonder-makers who've gathered around countless tables at *Inside Edge Foundation for Education* and *Mastery Circle International* meetings, you've woven a forty-year journey of transformation. Week after week, you arrived with hearts wide open, creating sacred spaces where our mutual quest for wisdom flowed over seventeen hundred renowned morning speakers and countless sparkling conversations.

To the thousands of members and attendees who dared to dream bigger, reach higher, and uplift others: You've built empires not just of business but of human connection and possibility. Your ripples of positive change continue to touch lives across the globe. May we forever remain curious learners, joyful seekers, and passionate creators, nurturing a presence of growth and wisdom where magic isn't just expected: it's created, shared, and multiplied in the expansive embrace of community.

To my second late husband, Ted (Theodore S.) Wentworth, for thirty-one years of alchemical adventure. Your wisdom, playfulness, and loving spirit still work their magic. Thank you for bringing more wonder into my world through my stepdaughter Kathryn Wentworth Purdy, her loving husband Court Purdy, and our cherished granddaughters Aidan and Caitlin Purdy.

To my brother Eugene Webb—some bonds transcend the need for words. You are my compass.

To Paul's and my extraordinary grandchildren, Peyton Paul Bursin and Faith Marie Bursin. I am proud you are our living legacy.

To my soul family, Tim Piering, Mary Olsen Kelly, Alice Blair Simmons, Tom Sewell, Candace Wheeler, Dori Schneider, Lynn Andrews, Nita Alvarez, Sharon Lindsay, Christina (Kiki) Johnson, and Dodie Bushee. You are my shining mirrors.

To Jack Canfield and Mark Victor Hansen, who chose me as their very first co-author in the *Chicken Soup for the Soul* series. You sprinkled powerful magic into the Inside Edge and throughout the world with your 500,000,000 copies sold.

To the brilliant Jim Poole and the team at *NuCalm*™, I am deeply grateful for the product, the mission, and the healing that is happening.

To Amanda Pisani, John Niendorff, Mary Erpelding, and Owen Korsmo—your early faith in my words made them materialize. You were midwives to my emerging voice.

To my ever-expanding circle of creative conspirators—Robin Mullin, Sachi Webb, Carolyn Norris, Deb Gaal, Marigrace Gleason, Mary Ann Halpin, Susan Murphy, Afton Blake, Valerie Larenne, Lana Fears, Siddiqi Ray, Ellen Wolfe, Rhonda Swan, Michale Gabriel, Pamela Shandel, Stede Barber, my very beautiful assistant Taya Crayk-Bonde, and the continuous and the continuous parade of enchanting souls who weave their way into my life. You remind me that one of life's greatest gifts is its endless capacity for surprise.

To my editor Mimi Safiyah and all the team at Ignite Publishing™, thank you for your amazing work and dedication throughout this process.

Publisher's Note

As the founder of *Ignite Publishing*™ and co-author of *Expect Magic*, I've had the honor of collaborating with some of the world's most inspiring voices. But every once in a while, a project comes along that touches you in a way that's impossible to put into words. This book and the journey of writing it with Diana Wentworth has been exactly that: a transformative experience that will forever hold a special place in my heart.

I believe that every author who comes into my life arrives for a reason: to teach me something I need to learn at the perfect moment and in the most profound way. Diana has been that gift for me. Her grace, wisdom, and generosity of spirit became a guiding light during the many months we spent bringing *Expect Magic* to life. From our very first conversation, it was clear that Diana wasn't just going to be an author in my life. I quickly realized she was a mentor, a guide, a friend, and a sage whose wisdom and lessons resonated deeply with my own journey.

Each chapter we crafted, every interview session, and all the heart-felt discussions we shared seemed to mirror exactly what I needed to hear at that precise time in my life. It was as though the Universe had orchestrated our collaboration to be a reflection of my personal growth. The lessons Diana imparted weren't just for the pages of this book. They were for me also. I found myself not only crafting her message but also channeling her words and wisdom from a truly magical place where creativity and spirit flowed in perfect harmony.

I am deeply honored to have contributed my voice and vision to this work and to have allowed my skills as a *Word Artist*™ to shine through these pages. Formulating Diana's stories with intention and heart has been a privilege I treasure, as it gave me the opportunity to weave words that not only reflect her journey but also resonate universally with those seeking magic in their own lives. This book represents the culmination of my passion for storytelling and my commitment to creating transformational works that Ignite the hearts and minds of all humanity.

This book is more than just a collection of stories and insights. It is a testament to the symbiotic connection that Diana and I shared, a connection rooted in mutual respect, love, and a deep belief in the power of magic and synchronicity. *Expect Magic* is the culmination of our shared experiences, woven together with the intention to inspire, uplift, and ignite the spark of possibility in every reader.

To Diana, thank you for your unwavering faith in me, your trust, and for being a radiant example of what it means to live with grace and expectancy. You've not only gifted the world with your stories, but have left an indelible mark on my heart. This journey has been nothing short of magical, and I am forever grateful for the wisdom you've shared and the friendship we've built.

To our readers, I invite you to embrace the magic that surrounds you. Let this book, woven in love, friendship, respect, and collaboration be your guide, and may you discover, as I did, that expecting magic isn't just a mindset. It's a way of life that has the power to transform the world.

With love and gratitude,

Lady JB Owen

Founder & CEO, *Ignite Publishing*™

Co-Author of *Expect Magic*

Diana von Welanetz Wentworth Author Bio

Photographer: Mary Ann Halpin

Diana von Welanetz Wentworth's life is woven with threads of love, curiosity, and a relentless pursuit of connecting people. Born in Beverly Hills, her journey from aspiring young woman to a *New York Times* bestselling author, television personality, and influential community leader is marked by passion, perseverance, and an unwavering belief in the power of community and joy.

Diana's literary legacy is expansive and impactful. She is the author of eleven award-winning books, including the popular romantic memoir *Send Me Someone: A True Story of Love Here and Hereafter.*

This memoir tells the poignant story of love that transcends life and death, highlighting Diana's ability to turn personal experiences into universal lessons of hope and resilience. Her significant contributions to the literary world also include co-authoring the third book in the renowned *Chicken Soup for the Soul* series with Jack Canfield and Mark Victor Hansen. This series has sold over 500 million copies worldwide.

Her television career began with her late husband, Paul von Welanetz, with whom she hosted a long-running series on cooking and entertaining from 1983 to 1985. This series, *The New Way Gourmet*, aired on the Lifetime Network and brought people together around the table, embodying Diana's heart's path of connecting people through food and shared experiences.

In 1985, during the height of the Cold War, Diana and Paul embarked on a transformative journey to the Soviet Union as part of a documentary project with notable figures such as Dennis Weaver, Mike Farrell, futurist Barbara Marx Hubbard, and author Alan Cohen. This trip, aimed at fostering grassroots dialogue between Americans and Soviets, deeply impacted Diana and Paul, prompting them to shift their business focus toward community and personal development. Upon their return, they founded The Inside Edge Foundation for Education, a weekly breakfast forum in Southern California. The Inside Edge became a pioneering platform for transformative speakers and thought leaders, helping launch the careers of celebrated authors like Jack Canfield, Dr. Barbara DeAngelis, Dr. Susan Jeffers, and Louise Hay.

Diana's ability to ask profound, introspective questions—what she calls "Quantum Questions"—has been a cornerstone of her personal and professional journey. These questions, laden with anticipation and expectation, have consistently led to transformative answers and opportunities. One pivotal moment of clarity came when Diana asked herself, amidst uncertainty about her future, "What unique talents do I bring to this world that will lead to a loving and prosperous career?" The answer, which struck her like a thunderbolt, was to write a cookbook. This epiphany led to her first cookbook, which won the "Cookbook of the Year" award and paved the way for a 15-year career in the culinary world.

Beyond her literary and television achievements, Diana continues to inspire and connect people through online courses, individual coaching, and hosting private and group sessions of "Tea With Diana." Her philosophy of using joy as a compass in manifesting one's greatest potential lives is a guiding principle she shares widely.

Recently, she became a spokesperson, alongside Tony Robbins, for *NuCalm*™, an app she describes as the most life-enhancing tool she has ever discovered.

Throughout her remarkable journey, Diana has consistently reinvented herself, navigating the loss of careers and the death of two husbands. Her resilience is a testament to her philosophy that beauty and growth often emerge from life's darkest moments. Inspired by figures like Rumi and Buddhist nun Pema Chodron, Diana advocates for embracing difficult emotions fully, without judgment, as a path to wisdom and resilience.

Diana's life is a testament to the transformative power of surrender, joy, and deliberate inquiry. Her mantra, "Joy is my compass," encapsulates her approach to life, inviting others to join her in exploring the limitless possibilities that lie beyond comfort zones.

As Diana continues to share her passion for adventure and aliveness, she extends an open invitation for others to release their grip on familiarity, embrace uncertainty, and trust in the boundless possibilities that await. Through her fearless passion and inspirational journey, Diana von Welanetz Wentworth reminds us of the profound beauty and joy that can be found in living a life guided by love, curiosity, and connection.

Lady JB Owen
Co-Author Bio

Photographer: Stacey Thompkins

L ady JB Owen is a world-class transformational leader, bestselling author, and fearless believer in the limitless possibilities that unfold when we expect magic in our lives. As co-author of *Expect Magic*, Lady JB's visionary insight, creative brilliance, and heartfelt storytelling helped bring Diana Wentworth's wisdom to life, turning personal experiences into a vibrant, transformative guide. Together, they crafted a book that invites readers to recognize the magic within themselves and the world around them.

Lady JB's collaboration with Diana was more than a co-writing experience—it was a synergy of kindred spirits, both deeply passionate about the power of expectancy, synchronicity, and the limitless potential of the human spirit. Through her words, Lady JB encourages readers to not just *believe* in magic but to live it, embrace it, and *expect* it in every facet of life.

When she's not igniting hearts through books and speaking engagements, Lady JB can be found cycling the globe to raise funds for *Inspiration Classrooms*™, her global charity project focused on transforming education and igniting literacy worldwide. Her cycling adventures are a testament to her commitment to creating positive change, one mile and one classroom at a time, reflecting her unwavering belief in the magic of possibility.

Lady JB Owen is also the Chief Humanity Officer™, visionary entrepreneur, global speaker, and the founder and CEO of *Ignite Publishing*™ and the *Ignite Humanity*™ movement. She is dedicated to helping individuals worldwide discover their unique greatness and live their best lives. As Chief Humanity Officer of *Inspiration Classrooms*, she is revolutionizing education and empowering communities through the power of literacy and learning.

Her true focus is on empowering others, which inspired her to create *Ignite Publishing*, the leader in empowerment publishing. A world-class speaker, 26-time bestselling author, and powerful business owner, Lady JB is committed to raising the vibration of the planet and igniting a billion lives through *Ignite*. She is passionate about helping individuals break through limiting beliefs, experience their own 'Ignite Moment™,' and shift their lives toward greater purpose and fulfillment.

Lady JB exemplifies a new paradigm of what's possible, motivating and inspiring her clients to create ripple effects of change that will IGNITE humanity. Her work with *Word Artist™* authors reflects her passion for bringing iconic books to life in the areas of human consciousness, self-empowerment, and thriving communities worldwide.

She is on a mission to ignite a billion lives with a billion words and has been called the voice of humanity, having published over 800 stories on her mission to *Ignite Humanity*. Find out more about her at www.jbowen.website or www.igniteyou.life. Let her help you bring your story to life.